# SO WHAT

**Taha Muhammad Ali** was born in 1931 in the village of Saffuriyya, Galilee. At 17 he fled to Lebanon with his family after the village came under heavy bombardment during the Arab-Israeli war of 1948. A year later they slipped back across the border and settled in Nazareth, where he lived until his death in 2011. An autodidact, he owned a souvenir shop now run by his sons near Nazareth's Church of the Annunciation. In Israel, in the West Bank and Gaza, and in Europe and in America, audiences were powerfully moved by Taha Muhammad Ali's poems of political complexity and humanity. He published several collections of poetry and one volume of short stories. His edition *So What: New & Selected Poems 1971-2005* (Bloodaxe Books, 2007) was a Poetry Book Society Recommended Translation. Adina Hoffman's acclaimed biography of Taha Muhammad Ali, *My Happiness Bears No Relation to Happiness: A Poet's Life in the Palestinian Century* (Yale University Press, 2009), won the 2010 Jewish Quarterly Wingate Prize.

# TAHA MUHAMMAD ALI

# SO WHAT

NEW & SELECTED POEMS
(WITH A STORY)
1971-2005

TRANSLATED BY PETER COLE,
YAHYA HIJAZI & GABRIEL LEVIN

BLOODAXE BOOKS

ISBN:    978 1 85224 792 8

This edition published 2007 by
Bloodaxe Books Ltd,
Eastburn,
South Park,
Hexham,
Northumberland NE46 1BS.

First published in the USA in 2006 by Copper Canyon Press.

**www.bloodaxebooks.com**
For further information about Bloodaxe titles
please visit our website and join our mailing list
or write to the above address for a catalogue.

Supported using public funding by
**ARTS COUNCIL
ENGLAND**

Book design & English composition: Valerie Brewster, Scribe Typography
Arabic typography & design: Aissa Deebi
Cover design: Neil Astley & Pamela Robertson-Pearce

This is a digital reprint of the 2007 Bloodaxe edition.

ACKNOWLEDGMENTS

Earlier versions of some of these poems were published in *Lyric, The Jerusalem Post, The Manhattan Review, Modern Poetry in Translation, The Palestine-Israel Journal, Parnassus, PN Review,* and *Radical Teacher.* A smaller edition of this book—*Never Mind: Twenty Poems and a Story*—was published by Ibis Editions (2000).

"Twigs" appeared in *World Masterpieces* (Pearson Prentice Hall, 2004).

Arabic versions of the poetry and fiction are drawn from the volumes *Al-Qasida al-rabi'a* (1983), *Dahiq 'ala dhuqun al-qatala* (1989), *Hariq fi maqbarat al-dayr* (1992), *Ila, khalifa, wa-sabi farashat mulawanat* (2002), and *Ma yakun* (2003). Taha Muhammad Ali's recent work first appeared in *al-Ahbar, Masharef,* and *Kull al-'Arab.*

Numerous people have contributed in one way or another to the making of this book and to bringing Taha Muhammad Ali's work to a wider audience. The author and translators would especially like to thank Adina Hoffman, Eliot Weinberger, Jim Haba, Shirley Kaufman, Michael Wiegers, Jeremy Zwelling, Seth Altholz, Naomi Shihab Nye, Edward Hirsch, Eve Grubin, Alice Quinn, Don Faulkner, Jo Page, William Kennedy, Robert Schine, Joshua Sherman, Esther Allen, Forrest Gander, Barbara Epler, Rick Chess, Michael Sells, Nancy Larson Shapiro, Eric Selinger, Aharon Shabtai, Walid Ayyub, Vivian Eden, Ulrich Schreiber, Beatrice Fassbender, Rainer Zimmer-Winkel, Roger Allen, Nili Gold, Kathryn Hellerstein, Eric Zakim, Nimr Mattar, Sylvia Fuchs Fried, Barry Goldensohn, James Chansky, John Rommereim, Saadi Simaawe, Yael Lerer, Anton Shammas, Martin Earl, Christopher Merrill, Stephanie and Ruti Design, Sinan Antoon, Libby Rifkin, Sasson Somekh, Salman Masalha, Naseem Awwad, Phillip Fried, Jawad Siyam, Siham Daoud, Nancy Coffin, and Nina Subin.

# Contents

# On Taha Muhammad Ali

Having found Taha Muhammad Ali's store on Casanova Street in the old quarter of Nazareth empty, I sat on one of the low, wicker-topped stools and let my eyes roam about the shop. The shelves running up to the vaulted ceiling were crammed with imitation pearl-studded scabbards, ceramic bowls of various shapes and sizes, colorful kaffiyehs, olive-wood camels, inlaid boxes, narghiles, postcards of the legendary church rising above the shops at the end of the narrow street.

This wasn't exactly what I had expected. Some months earlier, when I'd first tried to translate two of Taha Muhammad Ali's poems, I had been told by a friend, who was then editing an anthology of Palestinian poetry, that the poet was a dealer in antiquities. Muhammad Ali was born and raised, my friend had explained, in the village of Saffuriyya, located on the site of what had once been the ancient town of Sepphoris, and at the age of seventeen was forced to leave with his family for Lebanon, after his village was attacked by the Israeli army in the Arab-Israeli war of 1948. A year later he and his family slipped back across the border and, finding the village destroyed, eventually settled in Nazareth.

Muhammad Ali, I now realized, was the proud owner of a souvenir shop. The only objects that might have passed for antiquities were some old farming implements and, leaning against the wall in one corner of the room, the waist-high jug once used by villagers for storing grain.

—

A slim young man entered the shop and introduced himself as Nizar, the poet's son. Taha would soon arrive, he announced. For some time now he and his younger brother had run the store. Their father, Nizar added, would show up on occasion only to disappear into the nearby shops to sip Turkish coffee with his old friends. I wondered whether one of the shopkeepers wasn't the friend Muhammad Ali had spoken of several weeks earlier in Jerusalem, at the city's third international poetry festival. The poet had prefaced the reading of his poems by telling us, in halting Hebrew, "a little story." Many years ago, he said, he had started up a stand along the street leading into the Old City market in Nazareth where he would display small lacquered camels made of olive wood and sell them to tourists who came from all parts of the world to visit the Church of the Annunciation. A certain friend of his used to visit him at the end of his workday and sit on the wooden stool he'd set out for him, so he could enjoy looking at the foreign passersby. "I would ask him to listen to a poem I had written the previous night," Muhammad Ali told us,

> and he would refuse loudly: "I don't want to hear it! I'm tired and I want to rest." One day it occurred to me that I might "bribe" him, by offering him one of the small wooden camels in exchange for his listening to my new poem. When I stretched out my hand to offer him the camel, a not unmysterious smile came across his face, and he took the camel, put it in his pocket, and offered me—of his two ears—only half an ear, with which he listened to my poem, all the while directing his eyes and his other ear-and-a-half to the people who were coming and going on the street before him, without there appearing on his face any indication that he was listening to me at all.
>
> Time passed, and I continued to give my friend camels in exchange for his listening to each new poem that I wrote. On one of these afternoons, wanting to save myself a camel, I announced to my friend that Jean-Paul Sartre had visited Nazareth, and that the city council had invited me to participate in a reception for him where I met and spoke with him

at length. My friend cut me off abruptly and said: "I know all about it, and I read in the paper that you talked to him about his play *The Respectful Prostitute*. I've also been told that the municipality asked you to participate in the reception for Arthur Miller... But what has this got to do with our topic? Sartre isn't a poet. Arthur Miller has absolutely nothing to do with poetry and poets. And even if this French existentialist had been a poet, and the late Marilyn Monroe's husband had written poetry, what has that got to do with listening to your nonsense? I've come here to forget about my troubles and rest after a hard day's work... My friend, I don't feel like listening! But let's get it over with..."

I paid him his lacquered wooden camel and he put it in his pocket and listened grudgingly as I read him my latest poem.

One day I said to my friend: "OK... And what do you have to say about the Hebrew poet Natan Zach and his splendid beard? He came here with a writer-friend of his from Paris and bought a camel from me to give to his French guest..." My friend cut me off and said: "I don't see any connection between a great poet like Zach and you." And I quickly shut him up with the usual camel... which he put in his pocket, and then, without looking at me or offering any visible sign that he was paying attention to the words, he listened to the new poem I'd written the previous night.

Mostly I was afraid that the ongoing blackmail would use up all of my "capital" and one day empty the store, and I'd end up with neither camels to sell to the tourists nor anyone to listen to my poems.

Last week, to my great surprise, I was sent a Spanish literary journal with poems by Natan Zach and Taha Muhammad Ali on facing pages. And that same week I also received an invitation to participate in the international poetry festival in Jerusalem. I took the Spanish journal and the invitation, and went to my friend and told him: What do

you have to say now? Natan Zach and I in the same maga-
zine! And this is an invitation to read at a festival where
hundreds of people will hear my poems, including agents
and journalists and people from television.

My friend took my hand between both his palms and
looked at me directly with both his eyes and said: "Taha,
you're a wonderful poet! I tried to burn you to a crisp! I told
myself: 'If there's anything left after I've burned him, then
he's a real poet. But if he's lost in the clamor of the street,
and transformed entirely into ash and dust blown by the
winds, then there's no need to feel sorry for him, no need to
be sad about what he's written.' And thus, my friend, I took
part in your creation!"

The following day my friend came to me carrying a fairly
large cardboard box, and said: "And these, my dear friend,
are your camels! Safe and sound and yours once again!"

—

Taha Muhammad Ali entered the shop, his head rising ponderously
above a sharply stooped back. A large, clownish nose and jutting
jaw suggested the uneasy cohabitation of mirth and menace. Three
parallel furrows ran up from brow to crown in a face whose raw,
impacted vitality might have been painted by Francis Bacon. He
shook my hand vigorously before proposing that we drive to his
home, located in one of the neighborhoods of Nazareth. I soon
found myself sitting on the balcony of a two-story stone house
surrounded by densely planted fruit trees—a concentrated version
of the traditional Arab *bustan*—and by rosebushes and a huge scar-
let bougainvillea that rambled over the porch. Muhammad Ali's
home seemed to belong to another time and place in the generally
bleak mix of debris-strewn lots, pitted roads, and unfinished cinder-
block homes, some rising to four or five stories. The neighborhood
had seen better days, as its Arabic name, Bir el-Amir, "The Prince's

Well," suggested. Like most Arab neighborhoods, villages, and towns in Israel, Bir el-Amir suffered from overcrowding, a paucity of state-allocated municipal funds, and neglect.

It was here that we met, sporadically over the next few years, sitting on Muhammad Ali's balcony or, come winter, in the reception room adjoining his living room, to converse, in a mixture of English, Hebrew, and Arabic. But mostly I listened to the poet's animated, impassioned talk. Muhammad Ali is a born raconteur, and his talk—of his childhood in Saffuriyya, of his early years selling trinkets from a peddler's cart, of his visit to Lebanon in 1983 to meet a childhood sweetheart now living in a refugee camp—tended to spill over into poetry. Was this a poem or just another extempore story that I was hearing in the poet's excited accents? I was never quite sure. Muhammad Ali's talk had a certain self-propelling quality to it, one which I soon realized charmed, baffled, and exasperated even the most fluent of Arabic speakers.

Saffuriyya, or at least the village of his childhood, where myth and reality converged, shone in the poet's mind as a place of prelapsarian innocence and embodied, in Palestinian terms, that period before the "great catastrophe," *al-nakba*, brought about by the Arab-Israeli war of 1948 and the consequent shattering and exodus of the Palestinian community. In July of that year Muhammad Ali's village, which had sheltered local militiamen, was bombed by Israel Defense Forces (IDF) aircraft and then hit by artillery. Most of the villagers fled into the surrounding wadis and orchards, believing that the Arab Liberation Army would come to their defense. But the ALA was not forthcoming, and the inhabitants of Saffuriyya dispersed. Some made their way northward, to Lebanon, while others found temporary refuge in the neighboring villages of Kafr Cana and Reine. The poet and his family chose the northern route to Lebanon, where they spent a year before managing to return to Israel. By then, however, the IDF had leveled Saffuriyya, and the Israeli authorities had handed over to local Jewish collective settlements (moshavim and kibbutzim) thousands of dunams of fertile village land. Like many other former inhabitants of Saffuriyya, Muhammad Ali and his family settled in Nazareth, where he has remained for the last fifty years.

During one of my visits the poet drove me to what was left of Saffuriyya, now called Tzippori (derived from the noun "bird" in Hebrew and spoken Arabic). Only five kilometers northwest of Nazareth, situated on a wooded rise and surrounded by vast stretches of cultivated fields, traces of the village, which once boasted some four thousand Muslim inhabitants, were barely discernible in a few cactus hedges and tumbledown stone terraces. Tzippori is now a thriving moshav, or Jewish farming community. Muhammad Ali casually pointed from the window of his car at a couple of large, broken stones near some wild bramble bushes outside the driveway of a whitewashed suburban ranch house: "Our home was here," he said, and drove on. I cast a backward glance at the village and, farther up, at the archaeological site of Sepphoris, inhabited at one time or another by Canaanites, Persians, Greeks, Romans, Jews, Byzantines, Crusaders, and Muslims. The site had recently become a major tourist attraction, after magnificent mosaic floors were uncovered in what had been a Roman villa. The eighteenth-century citadel of the Bedouin ruler Zahir al-'Umar, which had served as a schoolhouse during Muhammad Ali's childhood, rose above the dusty shrubbery. Then dusk descended as we wound up the hills leading into Nazareth, the song of blackbirds rising from the darkening orchards behind us.

—

Perhaps because the poet is an autodidact whose formal education lasted only four years, the poetry came slowly. He had a family to support, and lived, like the entire Israeli Arab community, under martial law until 1966, and he describes the late fifties and sixties as a time when he would sell souvenirs to the Christian tourists during the day and study classical Arabic texts in the evening:

the pre-Islamic *Mu'allaqat* or "suspended" odes, *Kitab al-Aghani* (*The Book of Songs*), al-Mutanabbi, Abu Nuwas, the Andalusian Ibn Quzman, *A Thousand and One Nights,* and twentieth-century writers Taha Hussein, Badr Shakir al-Sayyab, Nizar Qabbani, and especially the Syrian Muhammad al-Maghut, who was, like Muhammad Ali, self-educated. Muhammad Ali had also taught himself English and read a great deal of American fiction, especially Steinbeck, Erskine Caldwell, and O. Henry. He was also reading the English Romantic poets and Poe, and, in translation, Chekhov and Maupassant. He published his first short stories in the fifties, long before publishing poetry. And well before the early seventies, when his poetry began appearing in various Arabic periodicals in Israel and abroad, the poet's tiny, unassuming souvenir shop on Casanova Street had become an informal meeting place for such leading literary figures as Michel Haddad, Jamal Qa'war, Samih al-Qasim, and the near-legendary Rashid Hussein—schoolteacher, journalist, translator, and poet. (Persecuted by both Arabs and Jews for his belief in coexistence—he translated into Arabic Israel's first national poet, H.N. Bialik, and into Hebrew, together with the Jewish poet Natan Zach, a collection of Palestinian folk poems—Hussein died, impoverished and alcoholic, in 1977, in a fire in his New York City apartment, where he had lived in exile since the late sixties.)

Muhammad Ali absorbed the lessons of the European- and American-influenced "free-verse movement," which burgeoned in the fifties in Lebanon and Iraq. The Beirut-based *Shi'r* magazine had become at the time the standard-bearer for a new poetry, advocating at once prosodic experimentation, literary and political engagement, and the interpretation of contemporary themes through the rediscovery of myths indigenous to the Middle East. Great emphasis was placed by poets such as Yusuf al-Khal and Adonis (Ali Ahmad Sa'id) on the idea of renewal, or, in archetypal terms, of rejuvenation—of death and rebirth as exemplified, for example, in the Tammuz fertility myth—and Palestine became a living symbol of a land turned barren that one day would become fertile again.

Dispossession, exile, and cultural marginalization—the sine qua non of Palestinian poetry, especially that written in the Arab diaspora—more often than not were treated symbolically, or even allegorically, and the figure of the Palestinian took on heroic dimensions (he was likened to Sinbad the Sailor, Ulysses, Harun al-Rashid, Lazarus, Houdini). Muhammad Ali's poetry, by contrast, eschews the heroic mode and is set in the context of everyday experience. His only semi-mythological figure, Abd el-Hadi the Fool, is an innocent dreamer "who gets on my anger's nerves / and lights the fuse of my folly." This doesn't mean that political and historical events are glossed over, but rather that feelings of collective humiliation, shame, rage, and disillusionment (augmented not only by the June war of 1967 and the Israeli invasion of Lebanon in 1982, but by the repeated sense of betrayal by the Arab world) are modified by a highly individualized voice grounded in the history and language of the Galilee, and tempered by the work of memory and the imagination.

The singularity of Muhammad Ali's poetry, and particularly his use of Arabic, needs some elaboration. Arabic poetry may have freed itself in the last half century from the trammels of an excessively formalized prosody and absorbed a wide range of modern techniques—from the high symbolism of *The Waste Land* to the radical disjunctions of French Surrealism—but it has also remained, on the whole, loyal in its use of both traditional meters and an elevated diction cast in the literary registers of *fus'ha* ("pure" or "clear" Arabic). In fact, what is called "free verse" in Arabic (*shi'r hurr*) is actually a flexible variant of the classical line employing quantitative meters and rhyme, but most often in a broken or irregular array. ("Free verse" as we know it in English—that is, nonmetrical, unrhymed verse—is called *shi'r nathr*, literally, prose poetry; the prose poem of the French and English tradition is referred to by still another term.) On the level of diction, every educated Arab child, in essence, grows up with two semi-independent linguistic systems: one spoken and particular to the region in which

he lives, and the other written, rooted in the Qur'an, and conse-
quently pan-Arabic. A Syrian visiting Morocco might have a hard
time making himself understood in the *souq* of Casablanca, but he
will have no difficulty reading the local paper. Newspapers, the
news on television, academic texts, philosophical tracts, novels,
poetry, are all written, for the most part, in *fus'ha* – a literary lan-
guage of great lexical and syntactic richness, but also one that is
inherently conservative. Its venerable rhetorical tradition and in-
flationary allure have not diminished to this day. Hence the very
real difficulty in writing an anti-rhetorical poetry that would tran-
scend the layers of literary convention that poets traditionally
manipulate. There is, in fact, something quietly subversive in de-
flating the language of declamation and reverting to a poetics of
essences, which is at once innocent of pomp and cunning in craft.
"For an Arab poet to be truly modern," writes Adonis, "his writing
must glow like a flame which rises from the fire of the ancient, but
at the same time is entirely new."

This is not to say that attempts to use colloquial speech in po-
etry and fiction haven't been made. Individual poets and writers,
among them the Egyptian Salah Abd al-Sabur and the Syrian
Nizar Qabbani, have experimented with dialect and the local ver-
nacular, and with rhythms that approximate the rhythms of com-
mon speech. But this has been done with caution and, in order
to legitimize their deviations from a purely literary idiom, poets
have often drawn on the traditional colloquial *zajal,* a form, by and
large satirical in nature, whose master was the twelfth-century Ibn
Quzman. Until very recently the use of the colloquial in poetry
has been associated, at best, with popular folk literature and tradi-
tional songs, and, at worst, with the actual corruption of the Arabic
language. Naguib Mahfouz, for example, the Dickens of modern
Arabic fiction, writes with considerable vehemence of his opposi-
tion to popular speech forms: "The colloquial is one of the diseases
from which the people are suffering, and of which they are bound
to rid themselves as they progress. I consider the colloquial one

of the failings of our society, exactly like ignorance, poverty, and disease."

Muhammad Ali writes a literary Arabic that occasionally incorporates or, as he puts it, "grafts" onto the classical forms certain elements of a quasi-colloquial and often idiosyncratic Arabic, along with — in some instances — full-fledged dialect when his characters speak. In contrast to the stylized, heightened diction of most of his contemporaries, Muhammad Ali's lower register anchors the poetry to a sense of place without ever sounding merely like dialect. That, in combination with the poet's nonmetrical, unrhymed verse (he writes solely *shi'r nathr*), has given rise to the perception of him by some readers and critics as a popular, or *'ammiyeh*, poet and storyteller whose poetry is removed from the strains of his younger Palestinian contemporaries Samih al-Qasim and Mahmoud Darwish, both of whom have written an engaged poetry of resistance in the most resonant tones of a metrical *fus'ha* — which in itself assures them an audience inside and outside of Israel, the West Bank, Gaza, and Jordan (and, paradoxically, beyond exclusively literary circles). But Muhammad Ali's seeming insularity within the Palestinian community should not be disparaged. Arabic poets and critics have pointed out that Muhammad Ali's originality (and even his relevance to the Palestinian cause) lies precisely in his blending of registers and employment of natural, homespun imagery—both of which contribute to the poetry's apparent simplicity while belying all along its complex sensibility. Saffuriyya may have been razed to the ground, but its mores, language, and landscape remain paradigms of durable hope in the poet's imagination. In effect the rhetoric and technique of Muhammad Ali's poetry constitute yet another means of clinging to his home and land, and of being a *samid* — a term coined by Palestinians in the late seventies and meaning one who holds on tenaciously to his land and its culture and perseveres in adverse times.

—

Written in a forceful, direct style, in short lines of varying beats, with a minimum of fuss and a rich array of images drawn primarily from village life, Muhammad Ali's poetry recalls in contemporary terms the work of the great modern Turkish poet Nazim Hikmet, as well as the Central and Eastern European poetry of Ungaretti, of Holan, of Różewicz and Herbert, and of Weöres and Juhász, poets who wrote with unflinching honesty as the lights dimmed in their native lands. Such poets replaced the "poeticisms" of their elders with a stark, emotional directness. Montale spoke of wanting to "wring the neck of the eloquence of our old aulic language, even at the risk of a counter-eloquence," a turn of phrase that seems particularly applicable to Muhammad Ali's own poetics. But the poet's spoken rhythms and lean diction also suggests the down-to-earth vitality and inventiveness of America's early modernist poets. William Carlos Williams comes to mind: "And in proportion as a man has bestirred himself to become awake to his own locality he will perceive more and more of what is disclosed and find himself in a position to make the necessary translations. The disclosures will then and only then come to him as reality, as joy, as release."

Muhammad Ali has bestirred himself awake, and in doing so he has released a complex of emotions of startling and often unexpected force. One may be charmed by the poet himself, the village chronicler and seller of trinkets, the self-educated poet who has described himself as "a camel fleeing the slaughterhouses, / galloping toward the East, / pursued by processions / of knives and assessors, / women wielding / mortar and pestle for chopmeat!" But the parallel thrust of Muhammad Ali's work is revealed in a harsh, often painful realism, in emotional desolation, and in telling images of desertion, ruin, and the sudden eruption of violence that act as a foil to any temptation to give in to mere folklore and nostalgia. Not infrequently pain, joy, bitterness, and hope are inexorably linked, as in "The Evening Wine of Aged Sorrow," or in the poet's marvelous story, "So What," where a child's walking barefoot for the first ten years of his life leads to cuts and scars from "daggers of splintered glass," and "thorns sharp as venomous stingers," but also to the unmediated, tactile exploration of his surroundings:

> I'd walk, stand, then walk in the water, which usually covered my calf, feeling against my bare legs and the flesh of my feet and the nerve-ends of my toes small pieces of metal, for the most part little coins with holes at their center, coins that had been lost by their owners and swept away by the water, or marbles, bullet casings, and old ladies' copper rings that had been thrown away by grandsons, and small keys, and sometimes bigger keys, in addition to crooked old nails, bent like the words of liars.

It is hard to think of another Palestinian poet of Muhammad Ali's generation who writes with such intimacy while skillfully modulating between the personal and the public spheres of life. Muhammad Ali speaks in what might be called a figurative plainness, reducing the traditional rhetorical flourishes of Arabic literature to a minimum. In "Empty Words," for example, he addresses his "little notebook / yellow as a spike of wheat," in a tone reminiscent of Waller as echoed in early Pound. Though here, too, pastoral fancy soon turns into unremitting, even brutal, sorrow, a sorrow that is at once private and communal as the poet alludes to the exodus of Palestinians from the Haifa seaport in 1948. The poetry may be acutely personal, but time after time it conveys the sense that happiness is not something that "flees / every which way, / like a partridge." It is of another order altogether, and must in the end ally itself to the aesthetic realm, and the natural world embodied in the Blakean "minute particulars" of Saffuriyya. Lightened by a touch of the trickster's wiles (*Fooling the Killers* is the title of the poet's second volume of poems), the poetry is at once lyrical and blunt, graceful and harsh in its veracities.

—

Invited once again to Jerusalem to read from his work in the spring of 1997, Taha Muhammad Ali prefaced his poems with another short tale. (Introducing his poems with a story, the poet explained, was like showing the animated trailers that used to be run before a feature film appeared on the screen.) This time the poet spoke not of wooden camels but of an old-fashioned mousetrap. The story went something like this: One day, back in 1941, Muhammad Ali's mother discovered a mouse in their home. She gave her son two piastres and told him to run off to the local shopkeeper in Saffuriyya and buy a mousetrap. Muhammad Ali returned with the mousetrap, which the shopkeeper had mentioned was rare and made only in Hebron, and at exactly five o'clock he heard the trap door click shut. "I then saw," the poet exclaimed, his wrinkles creasing in his troll-like face, "the most beautiful mouse, with green eyes and a belly white as cotton." Fifty years later, the poet's wife spotted a mouse in her Nazareth kitchen and implored her husband, "Taha, quick, fetch me a mousetrap." Muhammad Ali drove into Nazareth and was told that the sort of mousetrap he was looking for no longer existed, though someone had heard that they were still being made in Hebron, now part of the West Bank. A week later, it just so happened, the poet was scheduled to read his poems at the Hebron sports club. Muhammad Ali recited his poems and was then invited to a sumptuous lunch. At the conclusion of the meal he asked his new friends, "By the way, does anyone in Hebron sell old-fashioned mousetraps?" A young man said that he knew where they could be purchased, and he promptly drove the poet to one of the local stores where Muhammad Ali saw the exact same mousetrap he had bought for two piastres as a child. "Did you make these traps?" he asked the owner of the shop. "No," the man answered, "they were made by my father, Ziab al-Shantawi." Muhammad Ali paused, and then said to the Jerusalem crowd: "This was the very same name as the shopkeeper in Saffuriyya." And so he returned home with a new-old mousetrap, and the next day, he added, at exactly five o'clock the mousetrap clicked shut, and once more he saw "the same, beautiful mouse, with green eyes and a belly white as cotton…"

The audience of Israelis—and a handful of Palestinians—chuckled, uneasily perhaps, and somewhat beguiled, for all were now dislocated: aware that the poet had caught them in the snare of his words, though it was hard to know just how. Taha Muhammad Ali, too, was visibly shaken by the story, as Saffuriyya of half a century ago was suddenly, disturbingly present, while present and future seemed every bit as fragile as the past he had summoned to his poems.

G.L.
July 1999/2006

# A Note on the Translation

The poetry of Taha Muhammad Ali forgoes the incantatory cadences of much modern Arabic verse in favor of a more speechlike but nonetheless carefully constructed and musical currency. *Al-sahil al-mumtani'a* (a difficult, elusive, or even inscrutable simplicity) is the Arabic term for what is in effect his working method, and it requires of translators every bit as much attention, and as intense an effort, as does more conspicuously formal verse. The subtle linking of consonant and vowel, the creation of pulse and its alteration, the modulation of dynamics, register, and tone, are just a few of the technical elements that go into the work. If, however, the poet in English is a "maker" (from the Greek *poieein*, "to make or fashion," as in the Scottish *makar*), in Arabic he is the *sha'ir*, the one who knows through feeling (*shu'ur*). The combination of these two notions yields what is to my mind the most critical ingredient of good translation, and certainly the translation into English of poems like those in this collection: a deep-seated sympathy with the poet's artistry and the spirit it embodies.

Arriving at that identification through the translation of Taha Muhammad Ali's poetry has provided one of the fuller pleasures of my life as a poet, for the alloyed aspects of these versions go well beyond their prosody and timbre; they extend into the realm of politics, friendship, and cross-cultural understanding—and sometimes misunderstanding. The collaborative nature of this project has involved all of these elements—from my first coming across powerful Hebrew translations of a few of Taha Muhammad Ali's poems in the early nineties by Palestinian novelist Anton Shammas and poet Salman Masalha, to Gabriel Levin's rendering several of Muhammad Ali's poems into English via the Hebrew and French of an Arabic-speaking Lebanese Jew (Roger Tavor), to what in the end became our approach, with Yahya Hijazi, in the earlier and smaller edition of this volume, *Never Mind: Twenty Poems and a Story* (Ibis Editions, 2000). Yahya, Gabriel, and I made a selection of Taha Muhammad Ali's work, and I then translated that selection directly from the Arabic—consulting Yahya at all points along the way, and incorporating his invaluable observations and astute readings of the poems. Yahya helped me identify cultural elements to which I'd been deaf, and guided me through the rockier passages of the Arabic when the translation was in danger of running aground. I also adopted many of Gabriel's locutions in the cases where he had already translated a poem. Gabriel and Ibis editor Adina Hoffman then went over all the translations and made important contributions, Taha Muhammad Ali carefully reviewed the entire manuscript, and Gabriel wrote the introduction. To that earlier volume we have now added fourteen additional poems for this new Copper Canyon Press edition; the additions have been drawn from the poet's four volumes in Arabic, as well as from his most recent uncollected writing, which was published in a variety of Palestinian literary journals and newspapers. Small changes have also been made in the introduction and in some of the poems from the earlier book. We have also added a section of endnotes glossing Arabic terms in the poems.

—

Since the publication of *Never Mind*, Taha Muhammad Ali and I have traveled together a good deal, by plane, train, golf cart, car, and van, giving readings throughout the United States and in Europe and Israel. Taha's company is much like his poetry: his approach to people and prices, buildings and streets—to meals, engines, tension, napkins, and occasions of diverse sorts—is transformative. His window on the world is a joy to sit by, and response to his work has been, at times, overwhelming, cutting across lines of literary alliance, ethnicity, and religion, and in many respects restoring at least this translator's faith in poetry's ability, *pace* Auden, to make something happen.

What is that thing? "To evoke in oneself a feeling one has once experienced and having evoked it in oneself then… to transmit that feeling [by means of certain external signs so] that others experience the same feeling—this is the activity of art," wrote Tolstoy in 1898. "Art is a means of union among men."

Israelis, Palestinians, Chinese, Americans, Syrians, Jews, Druze, Hindus, Christians, and Muslims, all of us, when it comes to the Middle East, approach with often barely conscious or wholly unconscious suspicions, fears, and prejudices of one sort or another—at least some of which must be overcome before others can be heard and perhaps understood, before minds might be changed and new vision afforded. There are of course coolly logical or harshly economic or military ways to change minds and alter positions (and they are being employed as I write); but by far the most organic way, and possibly the most effective, is Tolstoy's—infection with feeling and shared experience.

In Taha Muhammad Ali's case that feeling and experience range widely, from catastrophe to splendor, and his art makes us remember that the conflict in Israel-Palestine involves not merely a clash of ideologies, as the pundits would have it, or a battle of competing national prides or claims to property, as others might see it, but, above all, a struggle to preserve an essential dignity. For in taking us back to the root of our most profound sense of belonging and being, Taha Muhammad Ali's poetry is neither innocent nor naive—it is radical in the extreme: radically human. As such, it speaks with surpassing eloquence, not only for his own people, but for all of us.

P.C.
May 2006

So What

# عَبدِ الهادي يُصارِعُ دَوْلَةً عُظْمى

في حَياتِهِ
ما قَرَأَ وَلا كَتَبَ .

في حَياتِهِ
ما قَطَعَ شَجَرَةً،
وَلا طَعَنَ بَقَرَةً .

في حَياتِهِ، ما جابَ سِيرَةَ النِّيويورْك تايْمْز؛
بِغيابِها .

في حَياتِهِ،
ما رَفَعَ صَوْتَهُ عَلى أَحَدٍ
إلّا بِقَوْلِهِ :
« تْفَضَّلْ . . .
وَاللهِ العَظيمْ غيرْ تِتْفَضَّلْ! »

—

وَمَعَ ذلِكَ،
فَهُوَ يَحيا قَضِيَّةً خاسِرَةً .
حالَتُهُ، مَيْؤوسٌ مِنْها،
وَحَقُّهُ ذَرَّةُ مِلْحٍ،
سَقَطَتْ في المُحيطِ .

أَيُّها السَّادَةُ!
إنَّ مُوَكِّلي، لا يَعْرِفُ شَيْئًا عَنْ عَدُوِّهِ .

# Abd el-Hadi Fights a Superpower

In his life
he neither wrote nor read.
In his life he
didn't cut down a single tree,
didn't slit the throat
of a single calf.
In his life he did not speak
of the *New York Times*
behind its back,
didn't raise
his voice to a soul
except in his saying:
"Come in, please,
by God, you can't refuse."

—

Nevertheless—
his case is hopeless,
his situation
desperate.
His God-given rights are a grain of salt
tossed into the sea.

Ladies and gentlemen of the jury:
about his enemies
my client knows not a thing.

وَأُوَكِّدُ لَكُمْ،
أَنَّهُ لَوْ رَأَى بَحَّارَةَ الْإِنْتِرْبَرَايْز
لَقَدَّمَ لَهُمُ الْبَيْضَ المَقْلِيَّ،
وَلَبَنَ الكيسِ!

تموز ١٩٧٣

And I can assure you,
were he to encounter
the entire crew
of the aircraft carrier *Enterprise,*
he'd serve them eggs
sunny-side up,
and labneh
fresh from the bag.

VII.1973

# تَحْذِير

إلى هُواةِ الصَّيْدِ
وَشُداةِ القَنْصِ!
لا تُصَوِّبوا غَدَّاراتِكُم
إلى فَرَحي!
فَهُوَ لا يُساوي ثَمَنَ الخَرطوشَة
( تُبَدَّدُ باتِّجاهِهِ )
فَمَا تَرَوْنَهُ
أنيقًا وَسَريعًا
كَغزَالٍ،
وَيَفِرُّ في كُلِّ اتِّجَاهٍ
كَديكِ حَجَلٍ:
لَيْسَ فَرَحًا.
صَدِّقوني –
فَرَحي
لا عَلاقَةَ لَهُ بالفَرَحِ!

١٩٨٨/٩/١٢

6

# Warning

Lovers of hunting,
and beginners seeking your prey:
Don't aim your rifles
at my happiness,
which isn't worth
the price of the bullet
(you'd waste on it).
What seems to you
so nimble and fine,
like a fawn,
and flees
every which way,
like a partridge,
isn't happiness.
Trust me:
my happiness bears
no relation to happiness.

12.IX.1988

# مُضاعَفاتُ عَمَلِيَّةِ اسْتِئْصالِ ذاكِرَة

في قاموسٍ لِلْأَحْلامِ
غَجَرِيٌّ، وَقَديمٍ،
شُروحٌ لِاسْمي،
وَتَفْسيراتٌ لِما سَأَكْتُبُ.

أَيُّ رُعْبٍ يَجْتاحُني
وَأَنا أَتَصَفَّحُ نَفْسي
في مِثْلِ تِلْكَ المَعاجِمِ؟!
أَنا هُناكَ:
جَمَلٌ هارِبٌ مِنَ المَسالِخِ
يَعْدو نَحْوَ الشَّرْقِ،
تُطارِدُهُ مَواكِبُ مِنَ السَّكاكينِ،
وَالجُباةِ،
وَالزَّوْجاتِ المُلَوِّحاتِ،
بِمَدَقَّاتِ الكُبَّةِ!

لا أَظُنُّ أَنَّني مُتَشائِمٌ
وَبِالتَّأْكيدِ
لا أُعاني مِنْ صَدْمَةِ كابوسٍ
قَديمٍ أَوْ غَجَرِيٍّ،
وَلكِنَّي، في وَضَحِ النَّهارِ،
حينَ أَفْتَحُ المِذْياعَ

## Postoperative Complications
## Following the Extraction of Memory

In an ancient Gypsy
dictionary of dreams
are explanations of my name
and numerous
interpretations of all I'll write.

What horror comes across me
when I come across myself
in such a dictionary!
But there I am:
a camel fleeing the slaughterhouses,
galloping toward the East,
pursued by processions
of knives and assessors,
women wielding
mortar and pestle for chopmeat!

I do not consider myself a pessimist,
and I certainly don't
suffer from the shock
of ancient Gypsy nightmares,
and yet, in the middle of the day,
whenever I turn on the radio,

أَوْ أُغْلِقُهُ،
أَتَنَفَّسُ حالَةَ جُذامٍ،
فِقْهِيٌّ وَتاريخِيٌّ.
أَشْعُرُ أَنَّ عُرى اللُّغَةِ،
تَتَهَرَّأُ في صُلْبي، وَعارِضَيَّ،
فَأَعْزِفُ عَنْ أَداءِ فُروضي،
في النُّباحِ واصْطِكاكِ الأَسْنانِ.

أَعْتَرِفُ
أَنِّي أَهْمَلْتُ تَمارينَ ما بَعْدَ
اسْتِئْصالِ الذّاكِرَةِ
لكِنِّي أُنْسيتُ،
حَتّى أَبْسَطَ أَساليبِ السُّقوطِ عَلى البَلاطِ،
مِنْ شِدَّةِ الإِعْياءِ.

١٩٧٣/٤/١٠

or turn it off,
I breathe in a kind of historical,
theological leprosy.
Feeling the bonds of language
coming apart in my throat and loins,
I cease attending
to my sacred obligations:
barking, and the gnashing of teeth.

I confess!
I've been neglecting
my postoperative physiotherapy
following the extraction of memory.
I've even forgotten
the simplest way of collapsing
in exhaustion on the tile floor.

10.IV.1973

# تُرُمْبوزَة في شَرايينِ النَّفْط

طِفْلاً،
سَقَطْتُ في الغُرْز
وَلَمْ أَمُتْ .
وَفي الجَابِيَةِ،
غَرِقْتُ يَافِعًا
وَلَمْ أَمُتْ .
وَمِنْ بَعْضِ عَادَتي
الآنَ،
يا حَفيظَ السَّلامَةِ،
أَنْ أَصْطَدِمَ بِكَتائِبِ الأَلْغَامِ،
عَلى الحُدودِ،
فَتَتَنَاثَرُ أُغْنِيَاتي،
وَأَيَّامُ شَبابي،
زَهْرَةً هُنا
وَصَرْخَةً هُناكَ،
دُونَ أَنْ أَمُوتَ!

—

ذَبَحوني
عَلى العَتَبَةِ
كَخَرُوفِ العيدِ
« تَخَثُّرٌ في شَرايينِ النَّفْطِ » . . .

# Thrombosis in the Veins of Petroleum

When I was a child
I fell into a pit
but didn't die;
I sank in a pond
when I was young,
but did not die;
and now, God help us—
one of my habits is running
into battalions of mines
along the border,
as my songs
and the days of my youth
are dispersed:
here a flower,
there a scream;
and yet,
I do not die!

—

They butchered me
on the doorstep
like a lamb for the feast—
thrombosis
in the veins of petroleum.

«بِسْمِ اللهِ» . . .
وَذَبَحُوني
مِنَ الأُذْنِ إلى الأُذْنِ
آلافَ المَرَّاتِ .
وَفي كُلِّ مَرَّةٍ
كَانَ دَمي يَتَأَرْجَحُ
كَقَدَمِ المَشْنوقِ
وَيَسْتَقِرُّ، وَرْدَةَ خُبَّيْزَةٍ
كَبيرَةٍ وَحَمْراءَ
كَاللّافِتَةِ البَحْرِيَّةِ
تُرْشِدُ السُّفُنَ
وَتُحَدِّدُ مَواقِعَ القُصُورِ وَالسِّفاراتِ .

—

وَغَدًا،
غَدًا يا حَفيظَ السَّلامَةِ
لَنْ يَدُقَّ جَرَسُ تِلفونٍ
في قَصْرٍ أَوْ مَبْغًى
أَوْ إمارَةِ خَليجٍ
إِلّا لِتَقْديمِ وَصْفَةٍ جَديدَةٍ
لإبادَتي .
لكِنِّي . . .
كَمَا تَزْوي وَرْدَةُ الخُبَّيْزَةِ
وَكَمَا تَتَوَقَّعُ الحُدودُ
لَنْ أَموتَ
لَنْ أَموتَ

*In God's name*
they slit my throat
from ear to ear
a thousand times,
and each time
my dripping blood would swing
back and forth
like the feet of a man
hanged from a gallows,
and come to rest,
a large, crimson mallow
blossom—
a beacon
to guide ships
and mark
the site of palaces
and embassies.

—

And tomorrow,
God help us—
the phone won't ring
in a brothel or castle,
and not in a single Gulf emirate,
except to offer a new prescription
for my extermination.
But...
just as the mallow tells us,
and as the borders know,
I won't die! I will not die!

سَأَبْقى شَرْنيخَة فولاذٍ
بِحَجْم مُوسَى الكَبَّاسِ
مَغْروسَةً في العُنُقِ
سَأَبْقَى بُقْعَةَ دَم
بِحَجْم الغَيْمَة
عَلى قَميصِ هذَا العالَمْ!

١٩٧٣/٩/٢٣

I'll linger on—a piece of shrapnel
the size of a penknife
lodged in the neck;
I'll remain—
a blood stain
the size of a cloud
on the shirt of this world!

23.IX.1973

# اَلْقَصِيدَةُ الرَّابِعَةُ
## «اليَمَامَةُ التي رَحَلَت بِقِطارِ الشِتاءِ»

أميرَةُ!

عِنْدَما يَرْحَلُ أحِبَّاؤُنا

كَمَا رَحَلَت

تَبْدَأُ في دَاخِلِنا هِجْرَةٌ لا تَنْتَهي

وَيَحيا مَعَنا يَقِينٌ

أنَّ كُلَّ ما هُوَ جَميلٌ

فينا وَمِنْ حَوْلِنا

ما عَدا الحُزْنَ

يَرْحَلُ، يُغَادِرُ

وَلا يَعُودُ.

فَأشْجَارُ الرُّمَّانِ

الَّتي كُنْتِ تُحِبِّينَ أزْهارَها

تَرَهَّلَت أغْصانُهَا

وَغَادَرَتْها الظِّلالُ

والطَّريقُ وَأشْجارُ الكينا

وَجَداوِلُ الماءِ

كُلُّها رَحَلَت

بَعْدَ رَحيلِك

وَلَمْ تَعُدْ.

وَفي الشِّتاءِ

تَأْتي طُيُورٌ غَريبَةٌ لاجِئَةٌ

فيها سُمَّانٌ وَفيها عَصافيرٌ،

أجنِحَتُها مُلَوَّنَةٌ

فيها طُيُورٌ جارِحَةٌ

## The Fourth Qasida

When our loved ones leave
Amira,
as you left,
an endless migration in us begins
and a certain sense takes hold in us
that all of what is finest
in and around us,
except for the sadness,
is going away—
departing, not to return.
The pomegranate trees,
whose flowers you loved,
drooped and their shade withdrew,
and the path, and the china bark tree,
and the brooks—
all departed
after you left
and won't return.
During the winter,
strange birds seeking refuge arrive,
among them quails
and songbirds with colorful wings,
and also birds of prey,

وَفِيها طُيورٌ رَقِيقَةٌ حَزِينَةٌ
تَأْسِرُ بِطيبَتِها
تَلْقُطُ الحَصَى وَالقَمْحَ
وَتَرْتَجِفُ مِنْ شِدَّةِ البَرْدِ
وَعُمْقِ الإِحْساسِ بِالغُرْبَةِ
لكِنَّها جَميعًا
تَرْحَلُ فَجْأَةً
تَأْتي فَجْأَةً في الشِّتاءِ
وَتَرْحَلُ فَجْأَةً مَعَهُ.

—

لَدَيَّ يا أَميرَةُ شُعورٌ غَريبٌ وَقَوِيٌّ
يَتَعَزَّزُ كُلَّ شِتاءٍ
لِيُصْبِحَ أَكْثَرَ قُوَّةً
وَأَشَدَّ غَرابَةً
فَأَنا أَشْعُرُ أَنَّكِ سَتَأْتينَ يَوْماً
مَعَ هذِهِ الطُّيورِ
سَتَأْتينَ يَمامَةَ زَيْتونٍ
يَمامَةً فاتِنَةً
يَمامَةً عَطِرَةً
يَمامَةً رَشيقَةً أَليفَةً قَلِقَةً
تَهْبِطُ عِنْدَ شَجَرَةِ الكَرَزِ مِنْ حَديقَتِنا.
يَمامَةٌ شُعورُها بِالبَرْدِ قاتِلٌ
إِحْساسُها بِالغُرْبَةِ قاتِلٌ
حَنينُها لِكُرومِ الزَّيْتونِ قاتِلٌ
يَمامَةٌ تَبْنَسِمُ وَفي عَيْنَيْها بَساتينُ حُزْنٍ
تَنوحُ وَفي هَديلِها بَقايا فَرَحٍ.

and some that are sad and frail
and hold you spellbound in their goodness
gathering pebbles and grain,
and trembling in the tremendous cold
and out of a sense of profound strangeness—
though all of a sudden together they leave.
They come as one in winter suddenly,
as with it they suddenly flee.


—


I have, Amira, a strange and powerful feeling,
which grows still stronger in winter,
becoming increasingly forceful
and strange,
and I sense that you'll arrive
one day with these birds,
an olive's dove—
enchanting,
sweet-smelling,
graceful and gentle,
and restless,
alighting near
the almond tree in our garden.
A dove whose feelings of cold are fatal,
whose sense of strangeness can kill,
whose longing for the olive
grove is lethal;
a dove who smiles,
her eyes holding gardens of sadness,
while joy's remains linger on in her coo.

أنا سَأَعْرِفُها بِمُجَرَّدِ أَنْ أَراها

سَأَعْرِفُ أَطْواقَ النَّكَبات

المُعَلَّقَةَ بِعُنُقِها الحَنون

سَأَعْرِفُ نَظَراتِها الرَّبيعِيَّةَ الصَّافِيَةَ

نَظَراتِها النَّدِيَّةَ

كَأَحْلامِ البُحَيْرات

سَأَعْرِفُ خُطُواتِها المُخْمَلِيَّةَ الخَجولَةَ

خُطُواتِها الرَّتيبَةَ

كَأَنْفاسِ أَشْتالِ الخَسِّ

وَسَأَعْرِفُ صَوْتَها اللَّيْلَكِيَّ المُتَفَرِّدَ

صَوْتَها العَذْبَ

صَوْتَها الَّذي ما سَمِعْتُهُ

إِلّا أَحْسَسْتُ أَنَّهُ قادِمٌ مِنْ مَكانٍ في أَعْماقي قَصِيٍّ

مَكانٍ في النَّفْسِ سَحيقٍ

ضائِعٍ وَمَجْهولٍ

هذا الصَّوْتُ الَّذي يَبْلُغُني

فَأُصافِحُهُ وَأُعانِقُهُ

قَبْلَ أَنْ يَصِلَ سَمْعي

لا أُخْطِئُهُ

أَسْتَطيعُ أَنْ أُمَيِّزَهُ

مِنْ بَيْنِ أَصْواتِ يَمامِ الدُّنْيا

وَقَدْ جُمِّعَ وَوُضِعَ في حَديقَةٍ واحِدَةٍ.

حينَ أَراها سَتَرْحَلُ كَفِّي

إِلى مَوْضِعِ القَلْبِ مِنْ صَدْري

لكِنِّي لَنْ أَدَعْها

تَرَى الدُّموعَ في عَيْنَيَّ

The minute I see her, I'll know her,
and recognize, too, catastrophes' rings
hanging from her tender neck.
I'll know her clear, springlike glance,
her dewy gaze
like the dreams of lakes.
I'll know her shy, velvety steps,
her measured paces,
like breaths taken by seedlings of lettuce.
And I'll know her sweet, singular, lilac voice,
which—every time I heard it—
I sensed was coming from deep within me,
a remote place within my soul,
lost and unknown—
this voice that reaches me
and which I greet
and embrace before my hearing stirs.
I will not mistake it,
for I can distinguish between
the voices of all the doves of the world
gathered together in a single garden.
And when I see her, my feet will set out
for the heart's site within my breast.
But I will not let her see the tears
welling up in my eyes,

لا دُموعَ الفَرَحِ بِها
وَلا دُموعَ الخَوْفِ عَلَيْها
وَلا دُموعَ أعْوامِ الحُزْنِ
وَسِنيِّ العَذابِ .
سَيُهَرْوِلُ دَمي فِي عُروقي
لِلِقائِها
وَالتَّسْليمِ عَلَيْها
وَالاحْتِفاءِ بِهَا
هِيَ أيْضاً سَتَعْرِفُنا
حُزْنُنا سَيَدُلُّها عَلَيْنا
انْتِظارُنا سَيَدُلُّها عَلَيْنا
أَلحَنينُ يَدُلُّها
وَالغُروبُ وَالوَجْدُ
أَللَّيْلُ يَدُلُّها
وَالغَمَامُ وَالعُشْبُ
سَتَدُلُّها الغَابَةُ
الفُصُولُ
وَالطُّرُقاتُ
وَالأَنْهارُ
سَتَدُلُّها عَلَيْنا
سَتَعْرِفُنا وَتَبْكي
تَتَذَكَّرُنا وَتَبْكي
تَلْقُطُ الحَصَى وَالقَمْحَ
وَتَبْكي
تَرْتَجِفُ مِنْ شِدَّةِ البَرْدِ

neither the tears of my joy for her,
nor the tears of my fear for her,
and not the tears of years of sadness,
nor my years of pain.
My blood will rush in my veins
to meet her then and welcome her.
And she will know us as well,
our sadness will lead her to us,
our anticipation will lead her to us,
the longing will lead her,
the evenings, the ardor.
The night will guide her,
and the clouds and grass
and the forest will show her the way,
the seasons and rivers
and paths—
all will guide her toward us.

And she will know us and cry,
remember us and weep,
gather the greens and grain
and sob,
tremble from the force of the cold

وَعُمْقِ الغُرْبَةِ
وَتَبْكي .
نَرْوي لَها عَنْ حُقُولِ الشَّوكِ
وَثِمارِ الحَنْظَلِ
وَنَشْكو لَها جِنايَةَ الرِّياح
نَحْكي لَها عَنْ بَراثِنِ الشَّتاتِ
عَنْ لُؤْمِ رَحَى اللَّيْلِ
وَجَوَى الأُمسياتِ
نَحْكي لَها عَنِ القَهْرِ
وَالمَرارَةِ وَالضَّياعِ
وَنُذَكِّرُها بِبَراعِمِ الزَّيْتون
فَتَبْكي وَتَبْكي .
هِيَ لا تُنْكِرُنا
لا تَفْزَعُ مِنّا
وَلا تَبْتَعِدُ عَنّا
لكِنَّها تَرحلُ فَجْأَةً
كَما جاءَتْ فَجْأَةً
فَالشِّتاءُ
الَّذي أَحْضَرَها مَعَهُ حينَ جاءَ
يَمُرُّ ذاتَ صَباحٍ
مِنْ حَديقَتِنا
مُسرِعاً كَالقِطارِ
فَتَهُبُّ مِنْ نَوْمِها
مَذْعورَةً تَبْكي
وَتَتَعَلَّقُ بِإِحْدَى شُرُفاتِهِ
وَتَبْكي

and the depth of strangeness,
and weep.
We'll tell her of the fields of thorn,
the colocynth fruit
and crimes of the wind,
the fangs of dispersal,
the mill of night and its cruelty,
the ardor of evening;
we'll speak to her of defeat,
of bitterness and the loss—
and remind her of the olive buds,
as she weeps on and on.
She'll neither find us strange nor fear us,
and she will not draw back from us,
but suddenly she'll depart
as suddenly she appeared,
and the winter that brought her
with it when it arrived
that morning will pass from our garden
swiftly like a train.
Waking from her slumber
in terror, then, she'll cry
and hanging from one of its coaches' windows
she'll weep,

تَبْتَعِدُ
وَالدَّمْعُ يَمْلأُ عَيْنَيْها الحَبِيبَتَيْنِ.

—

أَمِيرَةُ!
عِنْدَما يَرْحَلُ أَحِبَّاؤُنا
كَمَا رَحَلْتِ
تَبْدَأُ في دَاخِلِنا هِجْرَةٌ لا تَنْتَهِي
وَيَحْيا مَعَنا يَقِينٌ
أَنَّ كُلَّ ما هُوَ جَمِيلٌ
فِينا وَمِنْ حَوْلِنا
مَا عَدا الحُزْنَ
يَرْحَلُ، يُغَادِرُ، يَبْتَعِدُ
وَلا يَعُودُ!

١٩٨٣/٢/٢٠

28

withdrawing into the distance,
the tears filling her lovely eyes.

—

Amira!
When our loved ones leave us,
as you left,
an endless migration in us begins,
and a certain sense takes hold in us
that all of what is finest
in and around us,
except for the sadness,
is going away,
departing, not to return.

20.11.1983

# اَلْخُروج

اَلشَّارِعُ مُقْفِرٌ
كَذاكِرَةِ الرَّاهِبِ
اَلْوُجوهُ تَنْفَجِرُ في اللَّهَبِ
كَثِمارِ البَلّوطِ
وَالمَوْتى يَمْلأُونَ الأُفُقَ وَالمَداخِلَ .
ما مِنْ وَريدٍ يَسْتَطيعُ أَنْ يَنْزِفَ
أَكْثَرَ مِمّا نَزَفَ
وَما مِنْ صَرْخَةٍ يُمْكِنُها أَنْ تَرْتَفِعَ
أَكْثَرَ مِمّا ارْتَفَعَتْ .
لَنْ نَخْرُجَ!

وَالكُلُّ في الخارِجِ بِانْتِظارِ المَرْكَباتِ
المُثْقَلَةِ بِالعَسَلِ وَالرَّهائِنِ –
لَنْ نَخْرُجَ!
تُروسُ الضَّوْءِ تَتَفَطَّرُ أَمامَ الحَصْرِ
وَعَدَمِ التَّكافُؤِ .
وَالكُلُّ في الخارِجِ يُريدُ لَنا الخُروجَ .
لَنْ نَخْرُجَ!

عَرائِسُ العاجِ يَدْلِفْنَ خَلْفَ الخُمُرِ
في وَهْجِ السَّبْيِ، وَيَنْتَظِرْنَ
وَالكُلُّ في الخارِجِ يَنْتَظِرُ مِنّا الخُروجَ .
لَنْ نَخْرُجَ!

# Exodus

The street is empty
as a monk's memory,
and faces explode in the flames
like acorns—
and the dead crowd the horizon
and doorways.
No vein can bleed
more than it already has,
no scream will rise
higher than it's already risen.
We will not leave!

Everyone outside is waiting
for the trucks and the cars
loaded with honey and hostages.
We will not leave!
The shields of light are breaking apart
before the rout and the siege;
outside, everyone wants us to leave.
But we will not leave!

Ivory white brides
behind their veils
slowly walk in captivity's glare, waiting,
and everyone outside wants us to leave,
but we will not leave!

اَلمَدافِعُ تَجْتاحُ حَدائِقَ العُنّابِ
تُدَمِّرُ أَحْلامَ البَنَفْسَجِ
تُطْفِئُ الخُبْزَ، تُميتُ المِلْحَ، وَتُطْلِقُ العَطَشَ
يُشَقِّقُ الشِّفاهَ والأَنْفُسَ .
والكُلُّ في الخارِجِ:
« ماذا نَنْتَظِرُ؟ لَقَدْ مُنِعَ الدِّفْءُ وَصودِرَ الهَواءُ
فَلِماذا لا نَخْرُجُ؟ »
اَلأَقْنِعَةُ تَمْلأُ المَنابِرَ والمَباغي وَدورَ الوُضوءِ .
اَلأَقْنِعَةُ الحَوْلاءُ مِنْ شِدَّةِ العَجَبِ
لا تُصَدِّقُ ما يُرى
فَتَهْوي مَشْدوهَةً تَتَلَوّى
كَديدانِ الأَلْسِنَةِ .
لَنْ نَخْرُجَ!


وَهَلْ نَحْنُ في داخِلٍ كَيْ نَخْرُجَ؟
اَلخُروجُ للأَقْنِعَةِ، لِلْمَنابِرِ، والمُؤْتَمَراتِ!
اَلخُروجُ لِلْحِصارِ القادِمِ مِنَ الدّاخِلِ
الحِصارِ المُتَحَدِّرِ مِنْ صُلْبِ صَحاري البَدْوِ السّامِيّينَ
حِصارِ الأَشِقّاءِ المُلَطَّخِ بِطَعْمِ النَّصْلِ
وَرائِحَةِ الغِرْبانِ .
لَنْ نَخْرُجَ!


والكُلُّ في الخارِجِ يُغْلِقُ المَخارِجَ
وَيُبارِكُ الطّاغوتَ
يُصَلّي، يَسْأَلُ المَوْلى، وَيَرْجو القَديرَ
أَنْ نَموتَ .

١٩٨٣/٢/٥

The big guns pound the jujube groves,
destroying the dreams of the violets,
extinguishing bread, killing the salt,
unleashing thirst
and parching lips and souls.
And everyone outside is saying:
"What are we waiting for?
Warmth we're denied,
the air itself has been seized!
Why aren't we leaving?"
Masks fill the pulpits and brothels,
the places of ablution.
Masks cross-eyed with utter amazement;
they do not believe what is now so clear,
and fall, astonished,
writhing like worms, or tongues.
We will not leave!

Are we in the inside only to leave?
Leaving is just for the masks,
for pulpits and conventions.
Leaving is just
for the siege-that-comes-from-within,
the siege that comes from the Bedouin's loins,
the siege of the brethren
tarnished by the taste of the blade
and the stink of crows.
We will not leave!

Outside they're blocking the exits
and offering their blessings to the impostor,
praying, petitioning
Almighty God for our deaths.

5.11.1983

# شَرْخٌ في الجُمْجُمَةِ

حينَ تُوُفِّيَ مُدَرِّبُ المَدْرَسَةِ
سَكَّرَتِ البَلَدُ .
تَرَهَّلَتْ أَثْدَاءُ النِّسَاءِ
وَنَامَ النَّاسُ مِنَ العَصْرِ
مِنْ شِدَّةِ الحُزْنِ .

أَحْضَروا لَهُ الطَّبيبَ
فاهْتَمَّ كَثيراً بالبَطْنِ والدِّماغْ .
جَفَّفَ الدَّمَ عَنْ يَاقتِهِ،
وَأَخذَ مِنْ جُيُوبِهِ عَيِّناتٍ رَمَادِيَّةً،
وَزَّعَها عَلى أَفْرادِ الأُسْرَةِ
كَما يُوَزَّعُ الكَعْكُ
أَيَّامَ الخَميسِ .

رَثَاهُ رَجُلٌ
ذُو حَاجِبَيْنِ،
وَمِرْوَحَةٍ،
يَعْمَلُ ضَابِطَ إيقَاعْ .
قالَ فيهِ كَلاماً
نَزَّلَ السُّنونو مِنْ سابعِ سَمَاءْ
وَجَمَّدَ الدَّواءَ
في الحُلوقِ .

# Crack in the Skull

The town shut down
the day the school's
manager died…
Women's breasts went soft,
and the people went to sleep
in the late afternoon,
so great was their grief.

The doctor was summoned
and gave his full attention
to the stomach and brain,
wiped the blood
from the collar,
extracted ash-gray
samples from his pockets
and passed them out
among the members
of his family
like sweetmeats on Thursdays.

He was eulogized by a man
with bushy eyebrows, and a fan,
who works as a drummer.
The words he spoke in his praise
brought the swallows down
from the seventh heaven,
and made one's pills
thick in the throat.

ذَكَرَ أَهَمَّ أَسْبَابِ الوَفَاةِ:
شَرْخٌ في النُّقوشِ البيزَنْطيَّةِ
الَّتي تُغَطِّي جِدَارَ الجُمْجُمَةِ؛
أَوْرَامٌ في الجُمْلَةِ اللَّاتينيَّةِ
اليُمْنَى؛
تَعَبٌ، جوعٌ، وَتَشَرُّدٌ،
دُيونٌ، وَتَعَاطِي مُهْلِكَاتٍ.
صاحِبُ المِقْبَرَةِ،
نَفْسُهُ،
تَذَكَّرَ المَوْتَ.
بَصَقَ عَلى الدُّنْيا
وَقَدَّمَ الجَدَثَ مَجَّانًا.
أُغْمِيَ عَلى كَبيرِ الحُرَّاسِ.
لا شَيْءَ كَالفاجِعَةِ
يُعيدُ خَدَمَ المَقَابِرِ
إلى لُغَةِ الأُمِّ.
أَخَذَ المِسكينُ
يَشْهَقُ بالأَرْمَنِيَّةِ:
«سَأَحْميكَ!
سَأَحْميكَ، يا ابْنَ أَمَةِ اللهِ،
مِنَ القاقِ
وَالضِّباعِ المُرَقَّطَةِ. »

He mentioned the primary
causes of death:
a crack in the Byzantine inscriptions
lining the walls of the skull,
tumescence in the dextral
Latin clause,
fatigue, hunger, vagrancy,
debts and addiction to ruin.
Even the owner of the cemetery
thought about death
once again: he spat at the world
and offered the grave free of charge.
The head guard fainted.
There's nothing like a catastrophe
to bring a graveyard attendant
back to his mother tongue.
The poor soul
sobbed in Armenian:
"I'll protect you,
son of God's servant,
I'll protect you from the crows
and the spotted hyenas."

نَقَشوا عَلَى قَبْرِهِ مَواضيعَ إِنْشاءٍ
نَقَلوها مِنْ أَصْقاعٍ نائِيَةٍ
عَلى عَرَباتِ خَيْلٍ .
مَنَعوا التَّجَوُّلَ
وَطافُوا بِهِ البَراري وَالمُسْتَنْقَعاتِ
كَيْ يَحْفَظَهُ الرَّبُّ
عَنْ ظَهْرِ قَلْبْ!

١٩٧١/٨/١

On his headstone they chiseled
themes for a composition
brought from distant lands
in a horse-drawn wagon.
They imposed a curfew,
and took him around
from wasteland to swamp,
so the Lord
would know him by heart.

1.VIII.1971

# عَنْبَرٌ

آثارُنا دارِسَةٌ
رُسومُنا جُرِفَتْ
وَالبَقايا عافِيَةٌ
وَما مِنْ مَعْلَمٍ واحِدٍ
يُوحي بِشَيْءٍ
يَدُلُّ عَلى شَيْءٍ
أوْ يُومِئُ إِلى أَيِّ شَيْءٍ.
لَقَدْ تَقادَمَ العَهْدُ
وَتَمادَتِ الأَيّامُ
وَأَنا لَوْلا خُصْلَةٌ مِنْ شَعْرِكِ
شَقْراءُ كَرَحيقِ الخَرّوبِ
وَناعِمَةٌ كَشَذى الحَريرِ
كانَتْ فيما مَضى هُنا
تَغْفو كَفُلَّةٍ
تَخْفُقُ كَسَنا الفَجْرِ
وَتَنْبِضُ كَنَجْمَةٍ –
أَنا لَوْلا خُصْلَةُ الكافورِ تِلْكَ
ما شَعَرْتُ بِأَيِّ صِلَةٍ
تَشُدُّني إِلى هذِهِ الأَرْضِ!

–

# Ambergris

Our traces have all been erased,
our impressions swept away—
and all the remains
have been effaced…
there isn't a single sign
left to guide us
or show us a thing.
The age has grown old,
the days long,
and I, if not for the lock of your hair,
auburn as the nectar of carob,
and soft as the scent of silk
that was here before,
dozing like Arabian jasmine,
shimmering like the gleam of dawn,
pulsing like a star—
I, if not for that lock of camphor,
would feel not a thing
linking me
to this land.

—

اَلأَرْضُ خائِنَةٌ
اَلأَرْضُ لا تَحْفَظُ الوُدَّ
والأَرْضُ لا تُؤْتَمَنُ .
اَلأَرْضُ مومِسٌ
أَخَذَتْ بِيَدِها السِّنينَ
تُديرُ مَرْقَصًا
عَلى رَصيفِ ميناءٍ

تَضْحَكُ بِكُلِّ اللُّغات
وَتُلْقِمُ خَصْرَها لِكُلِّ وافِدٍ .
اَلأَرْضُ تَتَنَكَّرُ لَنا
تَخونُنا وَتَخْدَعُنا
والثَّرى يَضيقُ بِنا
يَتَذَمَّرُ مِنّا وَيَكْرَهُنا .
والوافِدونَ –
بَحّارَةٌ وَمُغْتَصِبونَ
يُزيلونَ الحَواكيرَ
وَيَدْفِنونَ الأَشْجارَ .
يَمْنَعونَنا مِنْ إطالَةِ النَّظَرِ
إلى زُهورِ البَرْقوقِ وَعَصا الرّاعي
وَيُحَرِّمونَ عَلَيْنا لَمْسَ البُقولِ
والعِلْتِ والعَكّوبِ !

ـ

This land is a traitor
and can't be trusted.
This land doesn't remember love.
This land is a whore
holding out a hand to the years,
as it manages a ballroom
on the harbor pier—
it laughs in every language
and bit by bit, with its hip,
feeds all who come to it.

This land denies,
cheats, and betrays us;
its dust can't bear us
and grumbles about us—
resents and detests us.
Its newcomers,
sailors, and usurpers,
uproot the backyard gardens,
burying the trees.

They keep us from looking too long
at the anemone blossom and cyclamen,
and won't allow us to touch the herbs,
the wild artichoke and chicory.

—

أَرْضُنا تُغازِلُ البَحّارَةَ

وَتَتَجَرَّدُ أَمامَ الوافِدينَ

أَرْضُنا تَتَوَسَّدُ فَخِذَ المُغْتَصِب

وَتَتَهَتَّكُ بِشَتَّى اللَّهَجاتِ

وَلا يَبْدو عَلَيْها ما يَرْبِطُها بِنا .

وَأَنا لَوْلا خُصْلَةُ شَعْرِكِ

الشَّقْراءُ كَرَحيقِ الخَرّوب

النَّاعِمَةُ كَشَذا الحَرير . . .

أَنا لَوْلا الكافورُ

لَوْلا النَّدُّ وَالرَّيْحانُ

وَلَوْلا العَنْبَرُ

ما عَرَفْتُها

وَلا أَحْبَبْتُها

وَلا دَنَوْتُ مِنْها .

—

جَديلَتُكِ

هِيَ السَّبَبُ الوَحيدُ

الّذي يَشْنُقُني إلى هذِهِ العاهِرَةِ!

١٠/٣/١٩٨٣

Our land makes love to the sailors
and strips naked before the newcomers;
it rests its head along the usurper's thigh,
is disgraced and defiled in its sundry accents;
there seems to be nothing that would bind it to us,
and I—if not for the lock of your hair,
auburn as the nectar of carob,
and soft as the scent of silk,
if not for the camphor,
if not for the musk and the sweet basil,
if not for the ambergris—
I would not know it,
and would not love it,
and would not go near it…

—

Your braid
is the only thing
linking me, like a noose, to this whore.

10.III.1983

# نَبيذُ أُمْسِياتِ الأَحْزانِ المُعَتَّقة

في المَساء
إذْ يَتَهَشَّمُ النَّهارُ
كَالجُمْجُمة
وَيَنْهارُ الزَّمَنُ
انْهِيارَ صَرْحٍ شامِخٍ
مِنَ الجُسورِ وَالقَناطِرِ،
وَتَتَناثَرُ اللَّحَظاتُ
كَزُجاجِ حَوادِثِ الطُّرُقِ :
يُبْعَثُ الأَسَى فَجْأَةً
تَتَجَمَّعُ الشُّكوكُ
تَنْطَلِقُ المَخاوِفُ
وَتَمُدُّ الهَواجِسُ أَعْناقَها
مُدَبَّبَةً
كَرُؤوسِ العَقارِبِ .

في المَساءِ يَكْبُرُ الحُزْنُ
يَتَرَعْرَعُ مَعَ كُلِّ نَفَسٍ
يَنْشَطُ مَعَ كُلِّ ذِكْرى،
وَمَعَ كُلِّ نَوْبَةِ حَنينٍ
يَرْبو وَيَزْدَهِرُ.
في المَساءِ يَتَراكَمُ في الصَّدْرِ
كَالطَّمْيِ؛ شُعورٌ بالعَتْمَة
وَإِحْساسٌ بالظَّلامِ :

# The Evening Wine of Aged Sorrow

At dusk,
as day is crushed
like a skull,
time collapses
like towering bridges
and vaults,
moments scatter
like shattered glass
from a car crash—
and despair
suddenly appears,
doubts gather,
fears are freed,
and worries stretch out their necks,
sharpened
like the scorpion's sting.

At dusk
sadness burgeons,
increases with every breath,
stirs with every memory,
and with each wave of longing
swells and blossoms.
At dusk a sensation
of darkness and gloom
floods the chest—
amassing like silt,
closing in

ظَلامٌ مُوصَدٍ كَالجُدْرانِ

ظَلامٌ يُحاصِرُ العُنُقَ

وَيُهاجِمُ الأَوْرِدَةَ

ظَلامٌ يَزْحَفُ بِبُطْءٍ

كَغُيومٍ هَدَّها التَّعَبُ

كَأَعْدادٍ لا حَصْرَ لَها

مِنَ الطُّيورِ العَمْياءِ

ضَلَّتْ طَريقَها

إلى حِضْنِ الغابَةِ .

وَالذي يَبْدو يا أَميرَةُ :

أَنَّ الطُّيورَ وَالأَنْهُرَ أَيْضًا

تَتَذَكَّرُ أَوْطانَها في المَساءِ .

فَمِنْ خِلالِ شِتاءٍ صَحْراوِيٍّ مُمْتِعٍ

يَمْلأُ القَلْبَ وَالذّاكِرَةَ

بالحَريرِ وَالبَراعِمِ

أَسْتَطيعُ أَنْ أَرَى لَوْعَةَ الطَّيرِ

وَشَوْقَ الأَنْهُرِ؛

أَسْتَطيعُ أَنْ أَلْمَحَ أَسْرابَ الفَراغِ

المُجَوَّفِ كالسَّراديبِ؛

أَسْتَطيعُ أَنْ أَشْهَدَ فَجيعَةَ المَزاوِلِ

وَهِيَ تَتَراجَعُ

كَسُفُنٍ أَضاعَتِ المَوانِئَ

كَجُيوشٍ فَقَدَتِ الماءَ وَالقادَةَ .

—

like a wall—
it tightens around one's neck,
assaults the veins,
slowly creeps like clouds
burdened with weariness,
like countless blinded birds
that have lost their way
to the heart of the forest.
And it seems, Amira,
the birds and rivers as well recall
their homeland at dusk.
And through the pleasant desert winter,
which fills one's heart and memory
with silk and buds,
I see the ardor of birds,
the yearning of rivers,
catch sight of the flocks
of emptiness, hollow
as any cellar.
I witness the calamity
of sundials in retreat,
like ships that lost
track of their ports—
or armies
that lost their leaders
and supply of water.

—

أَمّا أَنتِ أَيَّتُها الزَّيتونَةُ الأَسيرَةُ،
فَعِمي – يا شَجَرَةَ السَّبْيِ المُقيمِ، مَساءً
يا أَغْصانَ السَّفَرِ الدَّائِمِ
يا جِراحَ الرَّحْلَةِ الَّتي لا تَنْتَهي
جُفونُكِ المُخْضَلَّةُ
تُذَكِّرُني بِهِمْ
ظِلُّكِ المَقهورُ
يُذَكِّرُني بِأَبي
آه . . . يا والِدي
لَوْ كُنْتَ ما تَزالُ حَيًّا
تَمْضَغُ العَلْقَمَ وَتَنْتَظِرُ
تَغْضَبُ وَتَشْعُلُ وَتَرْتَدي العَباءَةَ
كَعادَتِكَ . . .
لَشَكَوْتُ لَكَ هذا الحُزْنَ الكافِرَ
الذي يَخْتَرِقُ صَدْري كُلَّ مَساءٍ
كَسَيْفٍ صيغَ مِنْ جَمْرٍ
كَنَهْرٍ قُدَّ مِنْ صَخْرٍ.

—

وَمَعَ ذلِكَ،
فَمُنْذُ أَنْ لامَسَتْ بَصَماتي هذا الفَضاءَ
وَأَنا أَحْلُمُ . . .

As for you, my captive
olive tree,
a splendid evening to you,
my tree of enduring captivity,
branches of the everlasting journey,
wounds of the endless wandering—
your moistened eyelids
remind me of them,
your vanquished shadow
recalls for me
my father.
Ah, Father,
if only you were alive,
still chewing your bitter gourd,
and waiting,
angry, coughing,
and wearing your robe,
as you would…
I'd complain to you
of this wretched sadness
which pierces my chest each evening
like a sword forged in burning coals,
like a river carved out of stone.

━

And, nevertheless,
ever since
I first caressed
the air of this world
with the tips of my fingers—
I've been dreaming…

أَحْلُمُ بِأَزْهَارٍ دافِئَةٍ
كَعُيون الأَطْفال
أَحْلُمُ بِشَوارعَ وَغاباتٍ
تُغَطِّي السُّفوحَ وَالمَواسِمَ
تَتَجاوَزُ حَدائقَ السّاعاتِ
لِتَتَغَلْغَلَ في فَضاءٍ عَفْوِيٌّ
مِنَ النُّجوم وَالسَّنابِل
حَيْثُ يَبْتَسِمُ لي المَساءُ
وَيَنْحَني يُواسِيني
كَجَدٍّ غايَةٍ بِالرَّأَفَةِ
ثُمَّ يَتَلاشى
خَلْفَ ضَجِيجِ قَوافِلِ النَّبيذِ وَالتَّوابِلِ.

—


أَيُّ شُعورٍ بِالفَرَحِ
حَزينٍ وَثَمينٍ
سَيَغْمُرُني
وَأَنا أَرى الأُمْسِياتِ
تَنْهَمِرُ ناعِمَةً حَنونًا
كَدُموع الأَخَواتِ
وَمِنْ ثُمَّ تَذوبُ
كَحُشاشاتِ حَبّاتِ البَرَدِ؟!

١٩٨٣/٥/٢٤

dreaming of flowers
warm as the eyes of children,
dreaming of streets and forests
that cover the slopes and seasons
and cross the hours' gardens
and seep through spontaneous space
made of stars and spikes of wheat,
a place where the evening
would smile at me,
leaning over to offer me comfort
like the gentlest of grandfathers,
before it fades
behind the tumult
of caravans of spices and wine.

—

What feelings
of sad and precious joy
come across me,
when I see the evenings
weeping softly, and mercifully,
as though with the tears of sisters,
then vanishing
like the last breath
taken by pellets of hail.

24.v.1983

# ضَحِكٌ عَلَى ذُقُونِ القَتَلَة

قاسِمْ!
تُرَى ... أَيْنَ أَنْتَ؟!
أنا لَمْ أَنْسَكَ
خِلالَ هذِهِ السِّنينَ
الطَّويلَة
كَأَسْوارِ المَقابِرِ
دائِمًا
أَسْأَلُ عَنْكَ العُشْبَ
وَأَكْوامَ التُّرابِ

أَأَنْتَ حَيٌّ،
بِعُكّازٍ وَهَيْئَةٍ وَذِكْرَياتٍ؟
وَهَلْ تَزَوَّجْتَ
وَلَكَ خَيْمَةٌ وَأَوْلادٌ؟
هَلْ حَجَجْتَ؟
أَمْ قَتَلوكَ،
عَلى مَداخِلِ تِلالِ الصَّفيحِ؟

أَمْ أَنَّكَ يا قاسِمُ
لَمْ تَكْبُرْ ...
وَاخْتَبَأْتَ عِنْدَ العاشِرَةِ؟

# Fooling the Killers

Qasim,
I wonder now
where you are...
I haven't forgotten you
after all these years,
long as the graveyard
wall is long.
I always
ask the grass of the field
about you, and the dirt paths.

Are you alive,
with your poise,
your cane, and memories?
Did you marry?
Do you have a tent of your own,
and children?
Did you make it to Mecca?
Or did they kill you
at the foot of the Hill of Tin?

Or maybe you never grew up,
Qasim, and managed to hide,
behind your mere ten years,

فَلَمّا تَزَلْ

قاسِمَ الصَّبِيَّ

الَّذي يَرْكُضُ وَيَضْحَكُ

وَيَقْفِزُ عَن السَّنَاسِلِ،

يُحِبُّ اللَّوْزَ،

وَيَبْحَثُ عَنْ عِشَاشِ العَصَافِيرِ؟

حَتّى إنْ كانوا يا قاسِمُ

قَدْ «فَعَلوها»،

وَقَتَلوكَ

فَيَقِيني أَنَّكَ «ضَحِكْتَ» عَلى قاتِليكَ

كَما «ضَحِكْتَ» عَلى السِّنِينِ.

فَهُمْ بِالتَّأْكيدِ

لَمْ يَجِدوا جُثَّتَكَ

عَلى كَتِفِ الطَّريقِ،

لَمْ يَعْثُروا عَلَيْهَا

لا في مَصَبَّاتِ الأَنْهُرِ

وَلا عَلى الرُّفوفِ

لا عَلى طَريقِ الحَجِّ

وَلا تَحْتَ الأَنْقَاضِ.

وَلأَنَّ أَحَدًا لَمْ يَرَكَ

وَأَنْتَ تُخْفي جُثْمانَكَ –

فَمَا مِنْ إِنْسِيٍّ

سَيَعْثُرُ عَلَيْكَ

ما مِنْ جِهَةٍ

سَتَقَعُ عَلى عَظْمَةٍ مِنْكَ

and you're still the same old Qasim,
the boy who runs around
and laughs
and jumps over fences,
who likes green almonds
and searches for birds' nests.

But even if they did it,
Qasim,
if, shamelessly,
they killed you,
I'm certain
you fooled your killers,
just as you managed
to fool the years.
For they never discovered
your body at the edge of the road,
and didn't find it
where the rivers spill,
or on the shelves
at the morgue,
and not on the way to Mecca,
and not beneath the rubble.

As no one saw you
concealing your corpse,
so no one will ever set eyes on you,
and no earthly breeze
encounter a bone of your body,

أَوْ إِبْهامٍ يَخُصُّكَ
أَوْ فَرْدَةِ حِذَاءٍ بِقِياسِ قَدَمِكَ .
لَقَدْ ضَلَّلْتَهُمْ يا قَاسِم!

—

لَقَدْ حَسَدْتُكَ دائمًا
يا قاسِم،
عَلى حُسْنِ اخْتِبَائِكَ
في « الغُمَّيْضَةِ . . . »
الَّتي طالَما لَعِبْناها
حُفَاةً في الأُمْسِياتِ
وَنَحْنُ أَطْفالٌ
قَبْلَ أَرْبَعينَ سَنَةً!

١٩٨٨/٨/٢٨

a finger of your hand,
or even a single shoe
that might fit you.
Qasim, you fooled them.

      —

I always envied you, Qasim,
your skill at hiding
in the games of hide-and-seek we played—
barefoot at dusk—forty years ago—
when we were little boys.

28.VIII.1988

# لَمْ يَكُنْ!

نَحْنُ لَمْ نَبْكِ
ساعَةَ الوَداعِ .
فَلَدَيْنا
لَمْ يَكُنْ وَقْتٌ
وَلا دَمْعٌ
وَلَمْ يَكُنْ وَداعٌ .
نَحْنُ لَمْ نُدْرِكْ
لَحْظَةَ الوَداعِ
أَنَّهُ الوَداعُ
فَأَنَّى لَنا البُكاءُ؟
وَنَحْنُ لَمْ نَسْهَرْ
( وَلَمْ نَغْفُ )
لَيْلَةَ الرَّحيلِ .
لَيْلَتَها
لَمْ يَكُنْ عِنْدَنا لَيْلٌ
وَلا نارٌ
وَلَمْ يَطْلَعِ القَمَرْ .
لَيْلَتَها أَضَعْنا النَّجْمَ
قِنْديلُنا ضَلَّلَنا
وَحَظُّنا مِنَ السُّهْدِ
لَمْ نُصِبْهُ
فَأَنَّى لَنا السَّهَرْ؟

١٩٨٨/١٢/١٦

## There Was No Farewell

We did not weep
when we were leaving—
for we had neither
time nor tears,
and there was no farewell.
We did not know
at the moment of parting
that it was a parting,
so where would our weeping
have come from?
We did not stay
awake all night
(and did not doze)
the night of our leaving.
That night we had
neither night nor light,
and no moon rose.
That night we lost our star,
our lamp misled us;
we didn't receive our share
of sleeplessness—
so where
would wakefulness have come from?

16.XII.1988

ثَلاثُ قَصائِد

### ١ . حَبْس

حينَ كُنْتُ طَليقًا
كانَ خَوْفي
يَلْتَفُّ حَوْلَ عُنُقي
كَأَفْعَى .
وَأَنْتِ كُنْتِ نَبْعَ الحُزْنِ .

أمَّا الآنَ
فَخُبْزُ خَوْفي نَفذَ
وَنَبيذُ حُزْني يَتَدَفَّقُ
مِنْ كُلِّ اليَنابيعِ .

### ٢ . إفْرَاج

حينَ كُنْتُ سَجينًا
كانَ اللَّيْلُ ثَقيلاً
كَالرَّصاص ،
وَالسُّكونُ كانَ صَلْدًا
كَالرَّحى ،
رَصاصٌ يَضْغَطُ الرَّحى

# Three Qasidas

I. IMPRISONMENT

When I was free,
my fear was wrapped
around my neck
like a viper!
And you
were the source of my sadness.

But now...
the bread of my fear has been depleted
and the wine of my sorrow
flows from every fountain.


II. RELEASE

When I was a prisoner,
nights were heavy
as lead
and the stillness was hard
as a millstone.
The lead pressed down against the stone,

وَرَحًى تَطْحَنُ الرَّصاصَ –
لا الرَّصاصُ يَذوبُ
وَلا الرَّحى تَتَفَتَّتُ.
وَأَنْتِ كُنْتِ المَلاذَ.

أَمَّا الآنَ . . . .
فَأَيُّ سَاقٍ
مَزَجَ الليلَ بِالسُّكونْ
دونَ أَنْ يَقْتُلَ صَمْت
دونَ أَنْ يَغْتالَ وَحْدَةْ؟

٣.  اَلحُلُم

فيما مَضى
كُنْتُ أَرَى في الحُلُم
أَنَّكِ رَاحِلَةٌ،
فَيَخْنُقُني الأَسَى.
وَلأَنَّ ذلِكَ كانَ حُلُماً
كُنْتُ أَسْتَيْقِظُ
فَأَفْرَحُ
وَيَمْلأُ القَمْحُ الظَّهيرَةَ.
فَأَنْتِ كُنْتِ الأَسَى
وَأَنْتِ كُنْتِ الفَرَحَ.

and the stone ground the lead
but the lead didn't dissolve,
and the millstone didn't crumble.
And you were my refuge.

But now...
What saqi
has mingled the night with stillness
without killing silence,
or slaying loneliness?


III. THE DREAM

Once
I'd see you departing
in the dream,
and sorrow would take
hold in my throat,
and because it was only a dream,
I'd wake
and joy would fill me...
and fields of wheat would fill the day.
And you were that sorrow,
and you were that joy.

أَمَّا الآنَ . . .
فَإِنَّني أَحْلُمُ
أَنَّكِ قادِمَةٌ،
فَأَفْرَحُ . . .
وَأَسْتَيْقِظُ لأُدْرِكَ أَنَّ ذلِكَ كانَ حُلُمًا
فَيَخْنُقُني الأَسَى
وَيَمْلأُ الشَّوْكُ الغَسَقَ.

١٩٨٨/٨/٢٠

But now…
I dream you're approaching
and joy comes through me,
and I wake to discover
it was only a dream,
and sorrow wells
up in my throat,
and dusk is covered with thorns.

20.VIII.1988

# لَيْسَ

أَيُّها الصَّيادُ العَجوزُ
يا جَدِّي!
أَتَوَسَّمُ فيكَ الطِّيبَةَ!
وَأَنا في مِثْلِ سِنِّكَ
كُنْتُ أُحْجِمُ عَنْ صَيْدِ سُمَّانِ المَساءِ
وَأَنا في مِثْلِ بَهائِكَ
كُنْتُ أُشيحُ بِوَجْهِيَ عَنِ الحَيَّةِ
أَثْناءَ تَجَرُّدِها مِنْ قَميصِها النّاصِلِ
وَأَقولُ :
«لَيْسَ!»

—

سَأُطْعِمُ كَلْبَكَ الذّابِلَ،
وَأَجْلِبُ لَكَ الماءَ وَالتَّبْغَ.
لَنْ أُنَبِّهَ الغُزْلانَ
وَالحَمامَ البَرِّيَّ
وَلَنْ أُبَلِّغَ المُفَتِّشينَ!
فَيا زَميلَ المُدَى
المُعَلَّقَةِ بِالأَحْزِمَةِ:
بَيْنَنا صَداقَةُ بَحْثٍ
عَنْ فِراخِ الحَجَلِ
في الجُيوبِ وَتَحْتَ القُبَّعاتِ.

## Never Mind

Grandfather,
old hunter,
in your face I read only goodness,
though I, at your age,
refrained
from hunting the evening quail,
and when I had your vigor
I'd turn away
from the snake as it shed its faded sheath,
and say:
"Never mind."

—

I'll feed your mangy dog.
I'll bring you tobacco and water.
I won't alarm the gazelles
or the wild doves
or say a word to the local inspectors.
The brotherhood of knives
hanging from belts
binds us in our search
for fledgling partridges
in pockets and underneath hats.

يا رَفيقَ العَطَشِ
والرِّثاءِ لِلأَرَانِبِ،
الَّتي ذَهَبَتْ بِالسَّذاجَةِ
وَلَمْ تَتْرُكْ لِمَخْلوقٍ
بَياضَ قَلْبٍ!
أَتَوَسَّلُ إِلَيْكَ :
دَعْني « أَتَنَزَّهُ »
عَلى مَرْمَى العِيارِ
مِنْ بُنْدُقِيَّتِكَ
في هذِهِ الحَواكيرِ المَهْجورَةِ
وَعِندَ بَقايا تِلْكَ السَّنَاسِلِ
إِسْمَحْ لِي
أَنْ أُسَلِّمَ عَلى هذِهِ التّينَةِ
وَأْذَنْ لي أَنْ أَقْتَرِبَ
مِنْ تِلْكَ الصَّبْرَةِ!
وَبَعْدَ رَحيلِ الحَصادِ
إِقْبِضْ عَلَيَّ
واذْبَحْني
بِخيطانِ المَصّيصِ الرَّفيعَةِ
المُنْسَابَةِ مِنْ حَقائِبِكَ وَأَكْمَامِكَ
انْسِيابَ الأَمْعاءِ
مِنْ بَطْنِ الدَّجاجَةِ!

١٩٨٨/٩/١٣

My comrade in thirst,
lamenting the rabbits
in their innocence,
who leave no creature
pure of heart—
I implore you:
Let me stroll
within range of your rifle,
among these deserted gardens
and ruined stone walls;
allow me
to greet this fig tree!
Let me draw near
to that particular cactus.
And then, after the harvest,
catch me
and slaughter me
with the fine threads
that dangle
from your pack and sleeves
like the guts from a chicken's belly!

13.IX.1988

# رُبَّما

في مَنامِي
رَأَيْتُ بِالأَمْسِ
أَنِّي أموتُ .
لَقَدْ رَأَيْتُ المَوْت
رُؤْيَةَ العَيْنِ .
شَعَرْتُ بِهِ
وَكُنْتُ فيهِ .
وَالوَاقِعُ أَنَّني ما كُنْتُ أَعْرِفُ
قَبْلاً
أَنَّ المَوْت
في أَكْثَرِ مَرَاحِلِهِ
يَنْسَابُ بِمِثْلِ هذِهِ السُّهولَة :
خَدَرٌ أَبْيَضُ دَافِىءْ
نَاعِمٌ وَفَضْفَاض
وَإِحْسَاسٌ بِالنُّعَاسِ لَذِيذْ .

عَلى العُمومِ
لا يُوجَدُ أَلَمٌ
وَلا رَهْبَةٌ .
رُبَّما
كانَ خَوْفُنا
المُبَالَغُ فيهِ
مِنَ المَوْتِ

# Maybe

Last night
in my dream
I saw I would die.
I saw death
eye to eye
and felt it—
was there inside it.
The truth is—
I've never known
before
that death
through most of its stages
would flow so easily:
a white, warm,
wide, and pleasant torpor,
a soothing sensation of lethargy.

Generally speaking,
there was neither
pain nor fear;
maybe
our excessive fear
of death

أَساسُهُ التَّصعيدُ المُكَثَّفُ

لِرَغْبَتِنَا فِي الحَيَاة.

رُبَّمَا.


لكِنْ

مَا أَعْجَزُ فِعْلاً عَنْ وَصْفِهِ

فِي مَوْتِي

هُوَ فَقَطْ

هذِهِ الرَّعْدَةُ، التِّلْقَائِيَّةُ،

المُدَمِّرَةُ،

الَّتِي تَجْتَاحُنَا

عِنْدَما نُوْقِنُ، وَنَحْنُ نَموتُ

أَنَّنا سَنُقْطَعُ عَنْ أَحِبَّائِنا

بَعْدَ قَلِيل –

فَلا نَراهُمْ

وَلا نَسْتَطِيعُ حَتَّى مُجَرَّدَ التَّفْكِيرِ فِيهِمْ!

١٩٨٨/٣/٢٢

is rooted
in an intense
escalation of desire
for life.
Maybe.

But in my death
the one thing
I can't describe
is the sudden shiver
that comes across us
when we know for certain we're dying,
that soon our loved ones will vanish,
that we will not see them ever again,
or even be able to think of them.

22.III.1988

# أَلْبَاشِق

١

إِذا اسْتَطَعْتُ يا حُزْنُ
يَوْمًا
أَنْ أَتَحَرَّرَ مِنْكَ،
فَأَنِّي سَأَشْعُرُ
حَتْمًا
بِغِبْطَةِ المُنْتَحِرِ
وَهُوَ يَتَحَرَّرُ مِنْ تَبِعَاتِهْ!
وَأَفْتَرِضُ
أَنَّنِي انْطَلَقْتُ مِنْكَ
فَجْأَةً
انْطِلاقَ أَسْرابِ الصَّدَى
مِنْ حُقولِنا
وَجَماجِمنا
فَما الَّذي سَيَحْدُثُ؟
ما الَّذي يَحْدُثُ
لَوْ تَمَكَّنْتُ مِنَ التَّخَلِّي عَنْكَ
الآنَ؟
هَبْنِي خَرَجْتُ مِنْكَ
في هذهِ اللَّحْظَةِ
خُروجَ السِّكِّيرِ
مِنَ الحَانَةِ —

76

# The Falcon

## 1

If ever,
sadness, it might
be in my power
to free myself
from you one day,
then I would feel,
decidedly,
the suicide's delight as he's freed
from all responsibility!
And imagine that I
were suddenly
released from you,
like flocks of the *Sada'*—
the death-owl—
being released
from our fields and skulls...
What would happen then?
What would happen
were I to abandon you now?
Suppose I were, at this very moment,
to leave you behind,
as the drunkard leaves the tavern—

فَما الَّذي سَأَخْسَرُهُ؟
يَكْفيني أَنَّني لَنْ أَحْزَنَ
بَعْدُ :
لَنْ أَحْزَنَ حينَ يَأْتي الشِّتاءُ
وَلَنْ أَحْزَنَ حينَ يَذْهَبُ الشِّتاءْ
لَنْ أَحْزَنَ عِنْدَما يَجيءُ الصَّيْفُ
وَلَنْ أَحْزَنَ حينَ يَرْحَلُ الصَّيْفْ
لَنْ يُحْزِنَني تَشَرُّدُ الأَنْهُر
وَلَنْ تُحْزِنَني غُرْبَةُ الطُّيورْ.
حَتى الأَزْهارُ
نَفْسُها
لَنْ تُثيرَ بي
لا أَلْوانًا مُبْهَمَةً مِنَ الأَسَى
ولا صُنوفًا غَامِضَةً مِنَ الحُزْنْ.


٢


أَيَّتُها الطُّيورُ
أَيَّتُها الأَزْهارُ
وَأَنْتَ يا نَهْرُ –
بَعْدَ أَنْ يَتَخَلَّى حُزْني عَنْكُمْ
لَنْ تَكونَ الأَنْهُرُ أَنْهُرًا
وَلا الطُّيورُ طُيورًا!
حَتَّى الأَزْهارُ
ذاتُها

what would I lose?
For me it's sufficient to simply
not know sadness any longer—
not know it as winter approaches
and not when it departs,
not when summer arrives,
and not when the season moves on.
The rivers' vagrancy wouldn't sadden me,
nor would the birds' being sent away.
Not even the flowers
themselves
would stir
the obscure shades of sorrow in me,
or the various sorts of melancholy
that always remain a mystery.


2


Birds,
flowers,
and you, O river—
after my sadness is freed from you,
rivers will no longer be rivers,
nor birds birds,
and even the flowers themselves

سَتَكُفُّ عَنْ أَنْ تَكونَ أَزْهارًا.
سَيُمْسِي النَّهْرُ
دونَ حُزْني
مُجَرَّدَ ماءٍ.
وَالزَّهْرُ سَيُمْسِي
مَحْضَ نَبْتٍ
دونَ أَسايَ.
أَلطَّيْرُ بَعْدي
سَيُدْرِكُها اللَّيْلُ
وَتَموتُ.
وَالطُّيورُ الَّتي سَتَبْقَى
بَعْدَ حَنيني
وَخَلْفَ وَحْدَتي –
بومًا هُنا
وَأَغربةً هُناكَ –
هِيَ لَيْسَتْ طُيورًا
وَلا هِيَ عَصافير.
إذْ... ما الطَّيْرُ
بِلا ذِكْرَياتي؟
ما الطَّيْرُ
بِلا شَوْقي
وَما الصُّدّاحُ؟
ما الطَّيْرُ خارِجَ حُرْقَتي؟
أَلْعَصافيرُ بِلا حُزْني
غابَةُ مَناقيرْ
وَأَجَمَةُ مَخالِبْ.

will cease being flowers!
For without my sorrow,
at the end of the day,
rivers will only be water,
and the flower
merely a plant—
without my grief.
Without me
the bird will be seized
by night and perish.
And those that remain
after my longing
and apart from my solitude—
a crow here,
a screech owl there—
won't be birds,
and not songbirds.
For… what is the bird
without my memories?
What is the songbird
without my longing,
and what is song?
What is the bird beyond my burning?
Without my sadness
the songbirds are only
a forest of beaks,
a thicket of claws!

أَلْعَصافيرُ بلا حُزْني
كُتَلٌ دَمَوِيَّةٌ
لا يُظِلُّها رِيشٌ
إلّا . . .
لِتُلاحِقَها الأَفاعي،
وَلا يَكْسوها زَغَبٌ
هَشٌّ، رَقيقٌ
كَغِلالةِ الرِّمالْ
إلّا . . .
لإغْواءِ البُزاةِ
وَاجْتِذابِ الصَّيَّادينِ!

٣

وَمَعَ ذلِكَ
فَالَّذي يَتَراءَى لي
أَنَّني فِعْلاً
سَأَتَخَلَّصُ مِنْكَ!
سَأَتَخَلَّى عَنْكَ أخيرًا
وَأَرْتاحُ!
أَتَخَلَّى عَنْكَ
لأَوَّلِ مَرَّةٍ.
سَأُغادِرُكَ
كَما يُغادِرُ القُرْصانُ قارِبَهُ!
لكِنَّني لَنْ أَدْفِنَكَ

The songbird without my sadness
is merely a mass of flesh;
it wouldn't be covered
by a single feather,
except…
for the adder's pursuit;
and no fine down would clothe it—
the sand's gown across the dune—
apart
from the kestrel's enticement
and the hunters' lure!


3

And still,
it seems
I really will
be freed of you—
that I'll leave you
and find rest at last!
For the very first time,
I'll give up
and abandon you
as the pirate abandons his ship.
But I will not bury you

فِي رِمالِ الشَّاطِئِ
كَما يَدْفِنُ لُصوصُ البَحْرِ
نُقودَهُم وَأَقْراطَهُم.
لِتَنْهَبْكَ الثَّعالِبْ
فَأَنَا لَنْ أَعُودَ إِلَيْكَ!

٤

وَلَكِنْ . . .
بِرَبِّكَ أَيُّها الحُزْنِ،
قَبْلَ أَنْ نَفْتَرِقَ
لِي عِنْدَكَ رَجاءٌ؛
قَبْلَ أَنْ تَرْحَلَ
كَمَنْ رَحَلُوا
لِي لَدَيْكَ طَلَبْ:
فَأَنَا أَخْشَى أَلّا أَراكَ
بَعْدَ أَنْ أُوَدِّعَكَ.
أَنا في الوَداعِ
أُعْجُوبَةٌ.
أَنا لَمْ أُوَدِّعْ شَيْئًا
مِنْ أَشْياءِ الدُّنْيا
إِلّا فَقَدْتُهُ
إِلى الأَبَدِ،
وَلَمْ أَمْدُدْ يَدِي
بِالوَداعِ لِمَخْلُوقٍ

in the sands of the shore
as the thieves of the sea
bury their earrings and coins.
I'll leave you to the foxes—
and never return.


4


And yet…
by God, my sadness,
before we part
I'd ask of you,
before you leave
as those who've already left us,
I have but a single request:
I fear that I won't see you
after I say farewell—
for when it comes
to saying farewell,
I am—in fact—something wondrous:
Every single thing I leave
in the world
is lost for eternity!
And I do not stretch
out my hand
in saying farewell to a creature

إلّا تَمَنَّيْتُ
عَبَثًا
أَلَّا أَمُوتَ قَبْلَ أَنْ أَراهُ!


٥


أُرِيدُكَ يا حُزْنُ
أَنْ تَكْشِفَ لِي عَنْ أَمْرٍ
يُحَيِّرُنِي .
لَنْ أَسْأَلَكَ
كَيْفَ قُيِّضَ لَكَ
أَنْ تَذْبَحَنِي
عَلى هذَا النَّحْوِ!
لَنْ أَسْأَلَكَ
مَا الغَايَةُ
مِنْ جَعْلِي هكَذا:
أَنْهارُ كَالمَمالِك
وَأَتَصَدَّعُ كَجُدْرَانِ البَرَاكِينِ؟
لَنْ أَطْلُبَ إِلَيْكَ
أَنْ تُفَسِّرَ لِي هَدَفَكَ
مِنْ جَعْلِي هكَذا:
أَتَبَدَّدُ كَالسُّحْبِ،
وَأَتَساقَطُ
كَمَلامِحِ النُّسُورِ؟
أُمُورٌ كَهذِه

without my wishing, in vain,
not to die
before I'd see it again.


5


I'd like you, sadness,
to tell me
something that perplexes me.
I will not ask you how
it is that I was destined
to be slaughtered in this fashion!
Nor will I ask
what your purpose is
in having made me so—
to fall like kingdoms
and crack like the walls of volcanoes.
I will not plead with you to tell me
why you'd have me
scatter like clouds
and collapse
like the eagle's features.
Matters such as these,

لا شَكَّ تَعْنِيني
لكِنَّني أَدْمَنْتُها
فَلأَدَعْها الآنَ تَغْفُو
مِثْلَما يَغْفُو الخَوْفُ
أَحْيانًا
وَكَما تَغْفُو البُذورُ!


٦


أَنا أَيْضًا
لَنْ أَسْأَلَكَ
مِنْ أَيْنَ جِئْتَ
وَلا كَيْفَ تَهَيَّأْتَ لي
أَوْ أَيْنَ وُجْهَتُكَ؟
فَقَدْ تَعَقَّبْتُكَ
مِرارًا
وَأَنْتَ غافِلٌ.
كَقَصّاصٍ بَدَوِيٍّ
تَتَبَّعْتُ خُطاكَ –
فَقُدْتَني دَوْمًا
إلى هُناكَ
إلى المَكانِ نَفْسِهِ
إلى الزَّمانِ ذاتِهِ
وَإلى اليَنابيعِ إيّاها!

undoubtedly,
concern me,
but I have become addicted to them
and now I'd like to let them rest,
as fear, sometimes, begins to doze
and seeds seem to drowse.


6


Also...
I will not ask
where you came from
how you prepared,
or where you are going.
More than once
I followed you
when you weren't paying attention.
Like a Bedouin tracker,
I followed your trail...
And always you led me there—
to that same place,
and that same time,
and to those very same springs!

أَنا حَتَّى
لَنْ أَسْأَلَك
مَتَى
أَيْنَ
أَوْ كَيْفَ بَدَأْت
تَسْتَقِرُّ عَلى راحَتي هكَذا:
بَاشِقًا أَليفًا
ذَاكِرَتُهُ مُمَوَّجَةٌ
كَبُكَاءِ البَحَّارَةِ؛
جَناحاهُ
فِي اللَّيل
خِنْجَرانِ أَزْرَقانِ؛
عَيْناهُ حَبيبانِ
وَجَفْناهُ زِنادانِ أَخْضَرانِ
يَتَوَسَّلان.

ما يُحَيِّرُني،
يَا حُزْني
أَنَّك أَكْبَرُ مِنِّي
أَعْمَقُ مِنْ يَقَظَتي
وَأَكْثَرُ بُعْدًا
مِنْ كُلِّ أَحْلامِي!

7

I won't even ask you
when,
where,
or how you came
to settle like this
in the palm of my hand,
a trained falcon
whose memories come
in waves like the sailor's weeping—
whose wings in the night
are blue daggers,
whose eyes are like two lovers,
their lids resembling
two green imploring arms.


8

What baffles me,
my sadness,
is why you're so much
greater than I am—
deeper than my wakefulness,
and more remote than all my dreams!

بَصَمَاتُكَ أَشَدُّ تَعْقِيدًا
مِنْ هُوِيَّتِي،
وَوَجْهُكَ صَحَارٍ
فَضْفَاضَةٌ
يَضِيقُ بِهَا الدَّرْبُ
وَتَلْفُظُهَا المَوانِيءُ.
مَا يُحَيِّرُنِي
أَنَّكَ أَكْبَرُ مِنْ يَوْمِي
أَكْبَرُ مِنْ أَمْسِي
وَأَكْبَرُ مِنْ غَدِي!

٩

فِي طُفولَتِي،
يا حُزْنُ،
رَأَيْتُ عُصْفورًا
تُطارِدُهُ أَفْعى.
أَلْعُصْفورُ كانَ قَعِيدًا،
خَلَّفَهُ السِّرْبُ
وَالخَوْفُ الَّذِي شَاهَدْتُهُ
يَتَفَجَّرُ فِي عَيْنَيْهِ
وَهُوَ يُحَاوِلُ الفِرَارَ
لا يُمْكِنُنِي أَنْ أَنْسَاهُ:
غَابَاتٌ، وَأَقْمَارٌ، وَبُحَيْرَاتٌ،
مَنَافٍ، جَدَاوِلْ،

Your fingerprints are more complex
than my identity.
And your visage resembles
a vast desert:
before it the path loses heart.
Ports refuse it!
What confuses me is
that you are bigger than my day,
greater than my past,
and larger than my tomorrow.


9

In my childhood,
sadness,
I saw a songbird
being attacked by a viper.
The bird had been maimed
and the flock had left it,
and the fear I witnessed
exploding in its eyes…
as it tried to flee—
I cannot forget:
Forests, moons, and lakes—
exile, streams,

وَمُرُوجٌ لا يَحُدُّهَا البَصَرْ –
كُلُّهَا كَانَتْ
تَتَكَدَّسُ عَلى عُنُقِهِ وَتَنْهَارُ
بِسُرْعَةِ البَرْقِ
مِنْ شِدَّةِ الْهَلَعِ!
مَذَابِحُ وَمُدُنٌ
كَانَتْ تَتَجَمَّعُ في نَظَرَاتِهِ
بِسُرْعَةٍ مُذْهِلَةٍ
وَهُناكَ تَخْتَرِقُ رُعْبًا
وَتَتَنَاثَرُ عَلى رِيشِهِ
وَصَوْتِهِ وَقَدَمَيْهِ!
هَلَعُ ذاكَ العُصْفُورِ
لا يُمْكِنُ أَنْ يَكُونَ
هَلَعُهُ وَحْدَهَ!
خَوْفُ ذاكَ العُصْفُورِ
لا يُمْكِنُ أَنْ يَكُونَ
خَوْفَ عُصْفُورٍ وَاحِدٍ.
خَوْفُ ذلِكَ العُصْفُورِ،
يَا حُزْنُ،
لا يُفْهَمُ إلّا أَنْ يَكُونَ
خَوْفَ السِّرْبِ
بِأَكْمَلِهِ.

and pastures the eye can't hold—
all were heaped up around its neck
and gave way,
unraveling in a flash,
so strong was its fright!
Massacres and cities
were gathered there in its gaze
with tremendous speed
and, in terror, were burning—
spreading across its feathers,
its cry, its legs!
That small bird's fear
cannot possibly be
its alone!
That songbird's fear cannot possibly
be the fear of a single bird!
The fear of that small bird,
my sadness,
cannot be fathomed except
as the fear of the flock as a whole.

١٠

يُحيِّرُني يا حُزْنُ
أنَّكَ في مُعْظَمِ الأَحْيانِ
تَخْتَلِطُ عَلَيَّ
فلا أعْرِفُكَ!
فلَكَمْ أنْكَرْتُكَ،
لكَمْ تَنازَعَتْني فيكَ الشُّكُوكُ
ساعةَ تَصْطَفُّ الأُمْسِيَاتُ
والطُّيُورُ والأَشْجارُ
في طَوَابِيرَ بَعيدةٍ
تُحَاذِي الأُفُقَ
كُلٌّ يَنْتَظِرُ حَظَّهُ مِنْكَ
انْتِظارَ المَنْكُوبِينَ للعَوْنِ
أيَّامَ الكَوارِثْ؟
لكَمْ أنْكَرْتُكَ
وَأنا أتَصَفَّحُ أثَرَكَ
حائِرًا بِكَ
مُتَرَدِّدًا بِأَمْرِكَ
أُقَلِّبُ بَقايَا عُشِّكَ
كَما تُقَلِّبُ بَقايا المَخْطوطاتِ؟
أَأنْتَ حُزْني الشَّخْصيُّ؟
أَأنْتَ حَقًّا
حُزْنُ شَخْصٍ واحِدٍ؟
أَيُعْقَلُ أنَّكَ حُزْني وَحْدي
وَأنا لا أَفْهَمُكَ
إلّا أنْ تَكُونَ حُزْنًا سِرِّيًّا

Yes, you baffle me, sadness,
in that, most of the time,
you've confused me—
for I haven't been able to recognize you!
And how often have I denied you...
How often have doubts contended with me
over you, when evening and birds
and trees fall in—
aligned like columns
in the distance toward the horizon,
all waiting for their portion from you
like the dispossessed awaiting aid
upon their day of calamity?
How often have I denied you
even as I was studying your traces,
bewildered by you,
unsure of you,
turning over
what remained of your nest,
as remains of ancient manuscripts
piece by piece are turned?
Are you my private sadness?
Are you truly the sadness
of a single person?
Is it conceivable
that you are mine alone—
for I cannot understand you
except to think that you might be
a secret sadness the flock

خَبَّأَهُ السِّرْبُ عِنْدِي؟
أَبِمَقْدُورِي أَنْ أُفارِقَكَ
وَأَنا لا أُدرِكُكَ
إلّا أَنْ تَكُونَ حُزْنًا مُطارَدًا
تَتَعَقَّبُهُ الحُنُشُ
وَتَتَرَبَّصُ بِهِ الحِرابُ؟
أَأَسْتَطِيعُ أَنْ أَتَخَلّى عَنْكَ
وَأَنا لا أَعِيكَ
إلّا أَنْ تَكُونَ حُزْنًا مَمْنوعًا
أَوْدَعَهُ الجِيلُ لَدَيَّ
أَوْصانِي بِهِ
وأتَّمَنَنِي عَلَيْهِ؟


١١


أَغْلَبُ الظَّنِّ،
يا حُزْنُ،
أَنَّكَ لَسْتَ حُزْنِي وَحْدِي.
وَما دُمْتَ حُزْنِي وَحُزْنَهُمْ
فَكَيْفَ يُمْكِنُنِي
أَنْ أَتَصَرَّفَ بِكَ
وَحْدِي؟


١٩٨٤/٤/٢٩

has hidden with me?
Is it in my power to leave you
when I barely know you
except as something stalked,
pursued by snakes
and anticipated by spears?
Could I really let you go
when I am not aware of you
except in your being
a forbidden sadness
the age has left me,
entrusted to me,
charged me to protect?


11

Most likely,
sadness,
you are not mine alone
and, so long as you are mine and theirs,
how could I possibly
do with you what I will?

29.IV.1984

# حَبلْ صَبْحَة

– بْتِتْذَكَّرْ يا أَبو مْحمَّدْ
بْتِتْذَكَّرْ لَمَّا صَبْحَة
بَقَرَةْ جارْنا «أبو هاشِمْ»
أَكْلَتِ الْحَبِلْ؟
بْتِتْذَكَّرْ كيف
وِهِي تْنازِعْ
ذَبَحوها؟
وَعَلى ضَيِّ القَناديلْ
سَلَخوها
وبِالبَلطَاتْ شيلاتْ شيلاتْ
قَطَّعوها؟

إِمْ هاشِم
نَصْبَتْ مَناحَة
لَمَّا السَّكاكين
نِزْلَتْ بْصَبْحَة
وَبَناتْها «عَيَّطوا».
الكُلّ حِزِنْ
وَالْكُلّ ساعَدْ
وَالْكُلّ رَدَّدْ:
«فَرِّقِ الْحِمِلْ يِنْشالْ!»
والْحارَة عَنْ بِكْرَةِ أَبيها
تْكاتَفَتْ

# Sabha's Rope

Do you remember, Abu Muhammad,
do you remember when Sabha,
our neighbor Abu Hashem's cow,
swallowed the rope?
Do you remember how,
as she was dying,
they slaughtered her,
and, by lamplight,
flayed her and then,
bit by bit, with axes,
hacked her into pieces?

Emm Hashem
sent up her wailing,
as the knives sliced
away at Sabha,
and her daughters wept.
Everyone grieved,
and everyone lent a hand,
insisting,
"We'll share the burden.
We'll manage."
All the neighbors
rushed together,
shoulder to shoulder,

واشْتَرَتْ لَحِمْ صَبْحَة!
بْتِتْذَكَّرْ...
والّا نِمِتْ؟

ـ لا ... أَنا فايِقْ،
طَبْعًا بْتْذَكَّرْ...
وَبَتْذَكَّرْ «كَمانْ»
إنُّو ما حَدَا ذاقْ قَطْمِة
مِنْ لَحِمْ صَبْحَة!
اللَّحِمْ انْشَوى
إنْقَلى، إنْسَلَقْ
والبَعِض دَقْ كُبَّة
لكِنْ ما حَدا ذاقُه!
النّاسْ حَسُّوا كَإِنِّهِنْ شَرَحوا شَرْحاتْ
مِنْ جُثَّةْ قَتيلْ،
وَكَإنُّو اللّي انْطَبَخْ
هو لَحِمْ أَبو هاشِمْ
وَلَحِمْ أَهِلْ «بيتُو».
النْفوسْ صَدَّتْ
وَكَبُّوه.
مُدَّة...
والبَلَدْ يُخْنُقْها
أَسى صامِتْ مْلَثَّمْ
مِثِلْ صوتْ أَبو هاشِمْ خِشِنْ
وإخْضَرْ
مِثِلْ عينينْ صَبْحَة الخُضُرْ.

102

without exception
to buy Sabha's meat!
Do you remember—
or have you fallen asleep?

No, I'm awake—
of course I remember,
and I remember, too,
that no one ever
tasted a piece of that meat!
It was grilled,
fried, cooked,
and minced for chopmeat,
but no one ate it!
The people felt
they were slicing into flesh
fresh from a cadaver,
as though it were Abu Hashem's body,
or that of his family,
being carved.
Men and women turned in disgust
and threw it away.

For a while,
the village was choked
in a muted sort of grief,
like Abu Hashem's hoarse voice,
and green as Sabha's eyes.

– شايِفْ يا أَبو مْحِمَّدْ،

كانَتْ بَلَدْنا مْليحَة.

صَحيحْ كانَتْ فيها أَوْقاتْ عَلْقَمْ

لكِنْ مَرارْها طيِّبْ

بِشْبَهْ مَرارِ العِلْتْ

وَأَطْيَبْ!

شايِفْ...

شو كايِني بَلَدْنا مْليحَة؟


– مْليحَة؟!

هَه!

قال « مْليحَة » ... قال

ولِكْ!

وكْتابِ اللهِ العَزيزْ!

أَنا مِسْتْعِدّْ وَبَفَضِّلْ

وَمِنْ كُلِّ قَلْبي موافِقْ

أَكونْ يومْها بَلَعِتْ حَبِلْ

أَطْوَلْ مِنْ حَبِلْ صَبْحَة

بَسْ نْكونْ

بْقينا بْبَلَدْنا!


١٩٨٨/٣/١٥


104

Don't you see, Abu Muhammad,
our village was pleasant.
It's true, there were hard times,
but the bitterness was good,
like chicory,
or better!
You see what I mean…
wasn't it pleasant?

—Pleasant?!
Ha!…
Pleasant, he says,… pleasant.
Let me tell you,
by the book of Almighty God
I swear to you,
I was prepared,
in fact I would have preferred,
and with all my heart I would have agreed,
to swallow a rope longer than Sabha's,
if only
we could have stayed in our village.

15.III.1988

# نَاقُوس مُرور الأربعين
## عَلى تَخْرِيب قَرْية!

الماضي يَغْفُو بِجَانِبي
كَمَا يَغفو الرَنِينُ
بِجَانِب جَده الجَرَس...!
والمرارةُ تَتْبعني
كما تتبع الصيصَان
أُمَها الدَجَاجَة...!
والأَفُقْ...
هذا الجَفْنُ المُطْبَق
على الرَمْل والدِمَاء
ماذا تَرك لكِ
وبماذا يَعِدُكِ!؟

٣٠/٨/١٩٨٨

# The Bell at Forty:
# The Destruction of a Village

The past dozes beside me
as the ringing does
beneath its grandfather bell.
And the bitterness follows me,
as chicks trail
after the mother hen.
And the horizon…
that eyelid tightly shut
over the sands and blood—
what did it leave you?
And, what hope does it hold?

30.VIII.1988

# كَلام

أَيُّها الدَّفْتَرُ الصَّغِيرُ
الأَصْفَرُ كَسُنْبُلَةٍ
وَالصَّامِتُ كَوَجْهٍ –
أَخْشَى عَلَيْكَ
مِنَ البَلَلِ وَالقَوَارِضِ
وَأَأْتَمِنُكَ على خَوْفِي
وَحُزْنِي وَأَحْلامِي
وَلا أَلْقَى مِنْكَ
سِوى العُقُوقِ وَالخِيانَةِ.
وَإلاَّ ...
فَأَيْنَ الكَلامُ
الَّذي أَقولُ مِنْهُ:
لَيْتَنِي صَخْرَةٌ
عَلى رَبْوَةٍ،
لا تَسْمَعُ وَلا تَرى
لا تَحْزَنُ وَلا تَتَأَلَّمُ؟
وَأَيْنَ المَقْطَعُ
الَّذي فَحْواهُ:
أَتَمَنّى أَنْ أَكونَ
صَخْرَةً عَلى رابِيَةٍ
يُفَجِّرُها الصِّبْيَةُ في الخَلِيلِ
وَيُهْدونَها إلى أَطْفالِ القُدْسِ
ذَخِيرَةً لِلأَكُفِّ وَالمَقالِيعِ؟

# Empty Words

Ah, little notebook,
yellow as a spike of wheat
and still as a face,
I've protected you
from dampness and rodents
and entrusted you with
my sadness and fear,
and my dreams—
though in exchange I've gotten from you
only disobedience and betrayal...
For otherwise where are the words
that would have me saying:
If only I were a rock on a hill...
unable to see or hear,
be sad or suffer!
And where is the passage
whose tenor is this:
I wish I could be
a rock on a hill
which the young men
from Hebron explode
and offer as a gift to Jerusalem's children,
ammunition for their palms and slings!

وَأَيْنَ العِبارَةُ
الَّتي أَوَدُّ فيها أَنْ أَكونَ
صَخْرَةً عَلى رابِيَةٍ
لأُشاهِدَ مِنْ هُناكَ
بَعْدَ مِئات السِّنينَ
جُموعَ الفاتِحينَ
المُلَثَّمينَ!؟

ثُمَّ أَيْنَ ما أَخُصُّ بِهِ حُلُمي
بِأَنِّي صَخْرَةٌ عَلى رابِيَةٍ
مِنْ رَوابي الكَرْمِل
حَيْثُ أَتَفَقَّدُ مَصادِرَ حُزْني
أُحَدِّقُ في المَوْج
أُفَكِّرُ بِالَّتي
مَضَى عَلى وَداعي لَها
عَلى رَصيفِ الميناءِ
في حَيْفا
أَرْبَعونَ سَنَةً
وَما أَزالُ
أَنْتَظِرُ عَوْدَتَها
مَعَ حَمائِمِ البَحْرِ
ذاتَ مَساءٍ؟

‏-

And where is the passage
in which I wanted
to be a rock on a hill
gazing out from on high
hundreds of years from now
over hordes
of masked liberators!

And where is what belongs
to my dream of being
a rock on a hill
along the Carmel—
where I call on the source of my sadness,
gazing out over the waves
and thinking of her
to whom I bade
farewell at the harbor pier
in Haifa forty years ago
and still…
I await her return
one evening
with the doves of the sea.

—

أَفَيَسْتَقِيمُ أَيُّها الدَّفْتَرُ الصَّغيرُ
الأَصْفَرُ كَسُنْبُلَةٍ
وَالصّامِتُ كَوَجْهٍ
أَنْ تَحْذِفَ ما حَذَفْتَ
تَطْمِسَهُ وَتُلْغِيَهُ
لِمُجَرَّدِ كَوْنِهِ
كَلامًا فارِغًا
لا يُخيفُ العَدُوَّ
ولا يُطَمْئِنُ الصَّديقَ؟

١٩٨٨/٩/٤

Is it fair, little notebook,
yellow as a spike of wheat
and still as a face,
that you conceal
what you cancel and erase,
simply because it consists
of empty words—
which frighten no enemy
and offer no hope to a friend?

4.IX.1988

# أماليد

لا المُوسِيقَى...
ولا الشُّهرةُ والثَّرْوَة
ولا حَتى الشِّعْرُ نَفْسُه
بِمُستطيعٍ أَن يعزّيني
عن قِصَرِ عمرِ الإنسان
وعن أن «الملك لير»
ثمانون صَفْحة ( وتنتهي )
وعن محض التَّصُور:
أنَّ المرءَ قد يُرْزَأُ
بإبنٍ عاقّ!

—

حُبي لكِ
هو العَظيم!
أما أَنا وأَنتِ والآخرون
فأغلبُ الظنِ أنّنا أُناسٌ عاديونْ!

—

قَصيدَتي
خارج الشِّعْرِ
لأنكِ خَارج النِّسَاء!

—

114

# Twigs

Neither music,
fame, nor wealth,
not even poetry itself,
could provide consolation
for life's brevity,
or the fact that *King Lear*
is a mere eighty pages long and comes to an end,
and for the thought that one might suffer greatly
on account of a rebellious child.

—

My love for you
is what's magnificent,
but I, you, and the others,
most likely,
are ordinary people.

—

My poem
goes beyond poetry
because you
exist
beyond the realm of women.

—

وهكذا...
إِسْتَغْرَقْتُ
الستين سنةَ كاملةْ
حتى أدركتُ :
أن الماءَ ٱلَّذُ الأشربةْ
وأنَّ الخُبزَ من الأَطْعِمةِ أَشْهَاها
وأنَّ لا قيمة حقيقية لأَي فنٍ
إلا إذا أَدْخَل البَهْجَةَ
إلى قَلْبِ الإِنْسَان!

—

بَعْدَ أَن نموتْ
وَيُسْدِل القلبُ المُتْعَبُ
أجفانَه الأَخيرةَ
على كُلِ ما فَعَلْناه
على كُلِ ما تَمَنَّيْناه
وعلى كُلِ ما حَلِمْنا به...
تَشَوقْنا إليه
أُو أَحْسَسْناه—
سَتكونُ الكراهيةُ
أولَ ما يَتَعَفَّنُ
فِينا!

١٩٨٩-٩١

And so
it has taken me
all of sixty years
to understand
that water is the finest drink,
and bread the most delicious food,
and that art is worthless
unless it plants
a measure of splendor in people's hearts.

—

After we die,
and the weary heart
has lowered its final eyelid
on all that we've done,
and on all that we've longed for,
on all that we've dreamt of,
all we've desired
or felt,
hate will be
the first thing
to putrefy
within us.

1989–91

# مُنْتَهى الحُب !

يُحَبِّبُني في العَيشِ
ما أَنا عَاجِزٌ
عن إدْرَاكِه . . .
عن نَوْشِه بقلم
أو إدارته على لِسَانْ!
وَيُحَبِّبُ لي الدُنيا والأَحلامَ
عند غابة الضوءِ تِلك
على ضِفاف الغُمُوضِ
من جَهْلِيَ المُخْجِلِ
بوجْهة الفُلْكِ
وغاية الرِحْلَةْ ـ
ما لا أَجْرُؤ على الإيحاءِ به
أو الايماء اليهْ!

وَحَتى . . .
لو خَلَتْ الأَيامُ
مما هو أعذَبُ
من بَحَّة الأُرغُولِ .
ومما هو أَشهى
من دِفءِ مواقِدِ الشتاءْ .
حتى لو خَلت مما هو أحلى
من « كِيفْ الحَال . . !؟»
تَضُوعُ من إبتسامةٍ فاتنةْ
فَسَأبقَى

118

# The Height of Love

What makes me love
being alive
is something I can't quite describe,
can't put into words with my pen
or utter aloud…
I love the world, and dreams
set in that forest of light
on the banks of the mystery
of my shameful ignorance
(concerning
the boat's destination
and the journey's goal)
—that at which
I haven't dared
hint or point…

And even if
the days were emptied
of all that was finer
than the reed-flute's rasp,
of all that is more desirable
than the warmth of the winter's fire,
even if they were emptied
of all that is sweeter
than "How are you?"
wafting up
from a winning smile,
I would go on

أُفَضِّلُ الحياةَ
على ألفِ موتْ!

لكنْ...
مأساةَ أَعْدَائِيَ
أنهم:
يَسْتَظْهِرون قَتْلِيَ
على عَجَلٍ
استظهار اللصِ المُسْرِعِ
لِصَلاته الكاذبةْ
فلا يدركونَ
لماذا
أبذلُ رُوحِيَ
كما يُبذَلُ النَقْدُ الزائِفْ؟!
كيف أَخْرج من دَمي؟!
وعُقُوداً
مِن مَلذَاتِي وحُبي
كيف أَسْفَحُها
في سَبِيلِ ما أُحبْ؟!

١٩٨٩/٨/١٠

preferring life
to a thousand deaths!

My enemies' tragedy,
however,
owes all to their rush
to rehearse my death—
as a thief is impatient
to get to his specious prayers.
They do not grasp
why
I spend my spirit
like counterfeit coins.
How I could leave
my blood behind?
And decades, decades
of delectation and love—
how could I shed them
for the sake of what I love?

10.VIII.1989

# لقاءٌ في مَطَارٍ أَرضُه وَدُود وَرَبُه مُحَايد!

سَألتِيني...
وكنا من ضُحى النَبع
مرة...
عائدَيْن
« ماذا تَكْره..
و(من) تُحِب؟!»

فأجبتُك
من خَلفِ أَهداب الفُجَاءةْ
ودَمي
يُسرعُ ويُسْرعْ
كظلِّ سحابةِ الزُرْزُورْ:
«أَكْرَهُ الرَحيلَ...
أُحبُّ النَبعَ والدَرْبَ
واعبُدُ الضُحى!»
فَضَحِكْتِ...
فأزهرَ لَوزْ
وشدَتْ في الايكِ أسرابُ العنادِلْ!

سؤالٌ!:
عُمرُه الآنَ عُقودٌ أربعةْ
يا لَلْجواب من السؤالْ
وجوابٌ:

# Meeting at an Airport

You asked me once,
on our way back
from the midmorning
trip to the spring:
"What do you hate,
and *who* do you love?"

And I answered,
from behind the eyelashes
of my surprise,
my blood rushing
like the shadow
cast by a cloud of starlings:
"I hate departure…
I love the spring
and the path to the spring,
and I worship the middle
hours of morning."
And you laughed…
and the almond tree blossomed
and the thicket grew loud with nightingales.

…A question
now four decades old:
I salute that question's answer;
and an answer

عُمرُه عُمرُ رَحيلِك
يا لَلْسؤآلِ من الجوابْ.

واليومَ:
يا لَلْمُحالْ!
ها نحن في مَطارٍ مُحايِدْ . . .
على شَفَا صُدْفةٍ
نَلْتَقِي!
وَيْحيْ . . .!؟
نَلْتَقِي . . .!؟
وها أَنتِ
تُعيدينَ السؤالْ؟!
يا لَلْمُحالِ من المُحَالْ!
عَرَفْتُكِ!
ولم تعرفينني.
« أهذا انتَ؟! »
ولم تُصَدِّقي.
وفُجْأَة . . .
إنْفَجَرَتِ تساؤلين:
« إن كنتَ أنتَ أنتَ
فماذا تكره
ومن تُحبْ؟! »

فأجبتُكِ
ودَمِي
يُغادِرُ الشُرفةْ . . .
يُسرِعُ ويُسرِعْ

as old as your departure;
I salute that answer's question…

And today,
it's preposterous,
here we are at a friendly airport
by the slimmest of chances,
and we meet.
Ah, Lord!
we meet.
And here you are
asking—again,
it's absolutely preposterous—
I recognized you
but you didn't recognize me.
"Is it you?!"
But you wouldn't believe it.
And suddenly
you burst out and asked:
"If you're really you,
What do you hate
and *who* do you love?!"

And I answered—
my blood
fleeing the hall,
rushing in me

كَظِلِّ سَحَابةِ الزُرْزُرْ:
«أَكْرَهُ الرَحِيلَ...
أُحبُّ النَبعَ والدَرْبَ
وأعبُدُ الضحى»

فَبَكَيتِ...
فَاطْرَقَت ورُودْ.
وتَعثرتْ بِحريرِ حُرقَتِها حَمائِمْ!

like the shadow
cast by a cloud of starlings:
"I hate departure,
and I love the spring,
and the path to the spring,
and I worship the middle
hours of morning."

And you wept,
and flowers bowed their heads,
and doves in the silk of their sorrow stumbled.

عَبْدِ الْهَادِي الأَهْبَل

« قَبْلَ نَهْشِ عَجِينِ جُمْجُمَتِي
بِكُلِّ مَنَاسِرِ العَالَمِ »
كُنْتُ أَهْبَلَ!
كُنْتُ غِرًّا
أَتَمَنَّى أَنْ أَطِيرَ
أَعْشَقُ الخَيْلَ والشِّعْرَ
وَأَحْلُمُ بِمَائِدَةٍ
دَائِمَةٍ . . .
مِنْ « خُرْجِ جَوْدَرْ »
كُنْتُ أَهْبَلَ!

وَبَعْدَ اغْتِصَابِ الضَّوْءِ
مِنْ ضَحْكَةِ الصُّبْحِ
فَجْأَةً
مُلِئْتُ بِالكَرَاهِيَةِ!
بَعْدَ وَأْدِ اليَنَابِيعِ
وَتَدْمِيرِ القَنَاطِرِ
اِجْتَاحَنِي اللَّهَبُ؛
بَعْدَ سَلْبِ الظِّلِّ
وَتَبْدِيدِ السَّنَابِلِ
بَعْدَ تَقْتِيلِ الحَمَائِمِ

# Abd el-Hadi the Fool

Before the dough of my skull was ravaged
by the buzzards of the world,
I was a fool!
I was naive...
and wanted to fly;
I loved horses and poetry.
I dreamed of a meal
that would last forever,
drawn from the wonders
of Jaudar's saddlebags,
a feast from *A Thousand
and One Nights*.
I was a fool!

But after the rape
of the light of morning's laughter,
suddenly,
hatred filled me.
After the springs were buried alive,
after the watercourses' destruction,
the flame swept through me.
After the pillaging of the shadow
and the sundering of the spikes of wheat...
after the murder of the doves...

شُحِنْتُ حِقْدًا قَاطِعًا
كَحَدِّ المَوْتِ
أَزْرَقْ .

لَمْ أَعُدْ أَهْبَلْ
وَاسْتَوْطَنَتْنِي المَرَارَةْ .
لِذا
تَرَانِي أَتَفَجَّرْ .
آوِي إِلى لَيْلِيَ
أَغْلِي .

أَتَمَنَّى حَرْقَ العَالَمْ !
أَتَمَنَّى طَعْنَهُ
فِي بَطْنِهِ
أَتَمَنَّى تَفْكِيكَ الكَوْنِ
بَعْدَ إِغْرَاقِهِ
وَأُعَاهِدُ
أَلّا أَمْنَحَ وَجْهَهُ
نَظْرَةَ وَدَاعٍ
عِنْدَ دَفْنِهِ !

بِحَارُ ظَلامٍ ثَقِيلٍ
تَقَضَّتْ
وَأَنَا أَنْتَظِرْ !
جِبَالٌ مِنَ اللَّيْلِ مَرَّتْ
وَأَنَا أَنْتَظِرْ !
عُهُودٍ بَطِيئَةٍ

I was charged with a sharpened hatred,
blue as the edge of death itself!

I'm no longer a fool,
and bitterness has settled
inside my soul.
Therefore…
I'm about to explode:
retreating into my night,
my blood boiling…

I wanted to burn down the world!
Wanted to stab it
in its soft belly,
and see it dismembered
after I'd drowned it.
And I vowed
I would not grant its face
the dignity
of a final farewell
at its burial…

Seas of heavy darkness
have drifted by,
and I am waiting.
Mountains of night have crept away,
and still I am waiting.
Ages, sluggish

كَنَبْضِ الكُهُوفِ
تَطَاوَلْتُ
وَأَنا أُغْمِضُ الطَّرْفَ
عَلى الهَدِيرِ
أُناجِيهِ
وَأَحْلُمُ بِالْقَاذِفَاتْ!

لكِنْ
رِدَّتي الكُبْرَى
أَنَّني
ما إنْ تَبْلُغُني
ضَحْكَةُ طِفْلٍ
أَوْ أُصَادِفُ
جَدْوَلاً يَنْتَحِبُ،
مَا إنْ أُشاهِدُ
زَهْرَةً ذَابِلَةً
أَوْ أَرَى امْرَأَةً جَمِيلَةً —
حَتَّى أُصْعَقْ!
يُغَادِرُني
كُلُّ شَيْءٍ
وَلا يَبْقَى مِنِّي
سِوَى
عَبْدِ الهَادي الأَهْبَلْ!

عَبْدِ الهَادي الَّذي
يَسْتَنْفِرُ غَضَبي
يُشْعِلُ فَتِيلَ جُنُوني

132

as the pulse of caverns,
drag on,
and I lower my eyelashes
on the raging,
communing with it
and dreaming of bombers!

However,
my great apostasy
is this:
no sooner does the laughter
of a child reach me,
or I happen upon
a sobbing stream,
no sooner do I see
a flower wilting,
or notice a fine-looking woman,
than I'm stunned
and abandoned by everything,
and nothing of me remains
except
Abd el-Hadi the fool!

Abd el-Hadi
who gets on my anger's nerves
and lights the fuse of my folly,

وَهُوَ يَبْسِطُ
ابْتِسَامَتَهُ الحَمِيمَةَ
لِمُعَانَقَةِ العَالَمِ
نَفْسِهِ،
وَمُصَافَحَةِ المَخْلُوقَاتِ
إِيَّاهَا!
لِمُعَانَقَةِ الأَبْرَارِ وَالأَشْرَارِ
جَمِيعًا
وَمُصَافَحَةِ الضَّحايا وَالجَلّادِينْ!
أَلَأَهْبَلْ!
يَحْضُنُ الدُّنْيا
كَأَنَّها مِخَدَّةٌ
يَحْضُنُ الدُّنْيا
كَأَنَّها ذِكْرَى خُطُوبَةٍ
أَوْ نَسَائِمُ حَقْلِ حِنْطَةْ!
يُلْصِقُها بِشَعْرِ صَدْرِهِ
كَأَنَّها ابْنَتُهُ
دُونَ أَنْ يَبْدُو عَلَيْهِ
أَنَّهُ يَعْبَأُ
بِدَمْعِهِ
المُنْهَمِرِ
نَائِحًا
مِنْ فَضاءِ مُقْلَتَيْهِ!

١٩٩٠/٥/٤

134

as he unfurls his warm smile,
embracing that very same world!
He shakes hands with creatures of various sorts,
embraces the righteous and wicked alike,
greets the victim and hangman as one.
The fool!
He hugs the world like a pillow;
he hugs the world as though it were
the memory of his own engagement…
or a breeze across a field of wheat!
He takes the world to the hair of his chest
like his daughter…
without there appearing on his face
any indication at all
that he's bothered
by the sobbing
or the tears
pouring from the sockets of his eyes!

4.V.1990

هُوَ ذا المِحْرَابُ ذُو الفُولاذِ السَّاقِطِ
وَتِلْكَ أُمِّي قَبْلَ أَنْ يُغَادِرَها النُّوَاحْ!


خَرَجْتُ لِتَوِّي مِنْ كَابُوسٍ أَرَانِي
«ضَبُعًا» عَارِيًا
مُخَطَّطَ الوَجْهِ والفَكَّيْنِ
يَغْتَصِبُ ابْنَةَ جِيرانِنا «فَوْزِيَّة»
عَنْ يَمِينِها أَبُوها كانَ قائِمًا يَبْتَسِمُ
وَخَلْفَهُ جِنِّيَّةٌ –
عَلى عُنُقِ مِحْرَابٍ فُولاذِيٍّ
آيِلٍ لِلسُّقُوطِ
مِنْ شَعْرِها
مُعَلَّقَةٌ!


أَفَقْتُ حَلْقِي يَابِسٌ
كَقِشْرَةِ جَوْزٍ
شَفَتَايَ مُصَفَّدَتانْ
أَتَمَنَّى لَوْ أَسْتَطِيعُ أَنْ أَفِرَّ مِنْ غَدِي
فِرَارَ النَّوْمِ مِنْ شُرْفَةِ الرَّأْسِ.


اللَّهُمَّ احْبِسْ عَنَّا هذَا،
احْبِسْهُ يَا رَبّ!

–

## This Is the Steel Mihrab About to Fall and That's My Mother, Before She Ceased to Mourn

Now I emerge from a nightmare
in which a naked hyena
with a striped face and muzzle
is raping Fawzeeya,
our neighbor's daughter.
Her father stands there
grinning by her side,
and behind him a maidenly jinn hovers,
hanging by her hair
from a steel mihrab about to fall.

I wake, my throat dry
as a nutshell,
my lips sealed shut,
and long to flee my future,
as sleep flees from the brow's balcony.

God, lock this away from us.
Lord, lock it away.

—

يَقِينًا إِنَّ اللَّوَاتِي أَرْضَعْنَنا
كُنَّ أَكْثَرَ تَفَاؤُلاً مِنَّا
فَتِلْكَ أُمِّي –
لَوْ عَادَتْ إِلَيْها قُدْرَتُها عَلى النُّوَاحِ
لَرَقَتْنِي –كاشِفَةً عَنِّي رَوْعي،
بِمُفْرَدَةٍ حَمِيمَةٍ وَاحِدَةْ:
« خِيرْ، يِمّا،
حِلِمْ خِيرٍ، يَا حَبِيبِي،
خِيرْ. والصَّلاةُ عَلى النَّبِيّ.
يَا سِيدْنَا البَدَوِي،
إِجْعَلُو خِيرْ! »

Certainly those who suckled us
were more optimistic than we are.
My mother, for instance:
if only her capacity for mourning
came back to her, would comfort me,
sweeping away all my fears
with a single, warm utterance:
"It will be all right, my dear,
it's a good dream, my child.
Bless our prophet Muhammad.
O Master Badawy,
please, make it good."

# تَوازُن

في سنة ١٩٤٨
كنا نَملُك ثَوْرًا
شَهْمًا
له قَرْنَان
كَبَاقِي الثِيرَان .
وكان لَدَيْهِم « تَرَاكْتور »
عَادِي
له جَنْزِير
كَبَاقِي التَرَاكْتورات!

# Balance

In 1948
we owned
a noble bull
with horns
like those of the other bulls.
And they
had an ordinary tractor
with a chain
like those
of the other tractors!

# فَلّاح

فَلّاحْ...
ابْنُ فَلّاحْ
بي سَذَاجَةُ الأُمّ
وَلي مَكْرُ
بائع سَمَك
لا أُوْقِفُ الجَرْشَ
وَفي حَلْقِ جاروشَتي
قَبْضَةُ حَبّ
وَلا أَكُفُّ عَنِ الحَرْثِ
ما بَقِيَ في خُرْجِي
مِنْ بذاري
مِلْءُ كَفّ!

٢٠٠٠/٦/٢٥

# Fellah

A peasant…
the son of a peasant:
there lies within me
a mother's sincerity
and a fishmonger's guile.
I will not stop
grinding
so long as in
my handmill's throat
a pinch of grain remains—
and I'll plow on
while the sack still holds
seeds my hand might sow.

25.VI.2000

# يَوْمَ صُعُودِ صابِر
## وَزَيْنَب إلى السَطْح

صَابِرُ الصَبي
والبِنت زَينب
والمخيمُ رَصَاصٌ وانْفِجَارات
صَعَدَا إلى السَطْح.
صَابِر قَفَزَ عَن السَطح
ظلِّ جَبينِه أَعلى من السطح
قَدَماه على الأَرض
وتدان في الأَرض...
أمامَ الجنود
والرَصَاصُ مَطَر!

زينب مَترسَت على السطح
صابر بعد أن مزّق قَميصَه
وكَشَفَ عن صدره
صاحَ بالجنود:
أطلقوا أطلقوا!

زينب القت زُجَاجتَها الفَارغَة
على سَيارةِ الجِيب
الدُنْيا رَصَاصٌ
دُخَانٌ ورَصَاصٌ

# Sahbr and Zeynab Ascend

The young boy, Sahbr,
and Zeynab, the girl—
while the camp
was all shots and explosions—
went up onto the roof.
Sahbr leapt along it
as above it the shadow of his brow rose.
His feet now firmly planted
in front of the soldiers,
bullets rained.

Zeynab took cover.
After he'd ripped open his shirt,
exposing his chest,
Sahbr shouted out to the soldiers:
"Shoot! Shoot!"

Zeynab threw an empty bottle
at the jeep
and bullets filled the air—
bullets and smoke.

من ثُقْبٍ صَغيرٍ صَغيرٍ

في صَدْرِ صابرِ الصَغيرِ

تَدَفَّقَ احمرارٌ زَغْلوليْ...

سائلٌ حارْ!

زينب لم تهبط عن السطح.

كثيرون في المُخَيَم شَاهَدُوا « زينب »

تَطير...

تَرْتَفِع ترتفع

وتَغيبْ

سُنُونُوة تغيبُ

في طيّات غَيماتِ

السَمَاواتِ السَبع

تَغيبْ!

٢٠٠١/٨/٢٤

146

From a tiny tiny hole
in young Sahbr's chest,
a warm redness flowed…
as though from a dove.
But Zeynab didn't descend.
Many in the camp saw her
flying…
rising higher and higher…
a swallow withdrawing
into the folds of the clouds
of the seven heavens,
fading away!

24.VIII.2001

# مِيْشيلْ

في مَرْسِيليا
المرأة الرّائِعة
التي أَقَمت في بيتها
طَوال أُسْبوع
إسمُها : مِيْشيلْ

—

زَوجُها الطَيب
يُدعَى ميشيل
وكَلبُها الأَبيض الجميل
إسمُه : ميشيل!

—

حَتى هَنْري
خادمُها العَجُوز
الذي « عَثرَتْ » أُمها عَليه
هائِماً . . .
في حدائق « إكْسْ »
بَعْد إعادته من فيتنام . . .
لا تناديه ميشيل إلا باسم :
ميشيل .

—

# Michelle

In Marseille,
the marvelous woman
in whose house I stayed
for a week
was called—Michelle.

—

Her kind husband
was named Michel,
and the name of her handsome
white dog was:
Michel.

—

Even Henri—
her servant of many years,
whom her mother had "stumbled on,"
aimlessly wandering
in the gardens of Aix-en-Provence,
when he was brought
back from Vietnam—
she called
Michel.

—

ذَاكِرتي سَتَحْتفِظ بالكثير
مما شاهدته
في جَنُوبِ فَرنسَا
لكنني بالتأكيد سأنتشي
كلما إِستَذْكرت
عذوبةَ عبارةِ ميشيل
في تَوِديعي:
ميشيل! *Au revoir*

In my memory I will preserve
much of what I observed
in the south of France;
but I will surely be swept away
whenever I
remember the day
and the sweetness of Michelle's saying
upon my leaving: *Au revoir,* Michel!

24.XI.1999

# لا لا . . يَابَا !

مُصْطَفى السَعيد
قال لأبنته أمينة :
« خَلَصْ ! . . .
تجوزِي أَبو طَالِب
أبو طالب سَبعْ
وأَنا أَعطيت كِلْمي !
دشْرِينا من الكَلبْ صُبْحِي . . .
صُبْحي كلب كلاب يا أَميني . . .
مَفْهُوم يابا ؟ ! »
أجابت أمينة والدَها :
« لا لا . . يابا، دَخيلَك
هاي جيزة العُمُر يابا،
صحيح ابو طالب سبع
لكن سبع ميّتْ يابا !
مفهوم يابا صُبْحي كَلبْ !
كلبْ كلبْ
لكن شَبْ
وصِحْتُو مْليحة يابا ! »

152

# No, Papa, Please!

Mustafa Sa'id
said to his daughter Amina:
"It's done!
You're marrying Abu Taleb!
Abu Taleb's a lion,
and I've given my word!
Forget about Subhi, that dog.
He's just a dog, Amina.
Do you understand?"
"No, Papa, don't. Please!
It's my *life*, Papa!
Abu Taleb's a lion, true—
but a dead lion, Papa!
I know Subhi's a dog!
A dog, a dog, I know…
but he's young, Papa,
and healthy!"

أَيْنَ؟

اَلشِّعْرُ يَكْمُنُ
في مَكانٍ ما
خَلْفَ لَيْلِ الكَلِماتِ
خَلْفَ غُيومِ السَّمَعِ
عَبْرَ عَتْمَةِ البَصَرِ
وَراءَ غَسَقِ الموسيقَى
ما بَطَنَ مِنْها
وَما ظَهَرَ.
أَمّا أَيْنَ مَكْمَنُهُ؟
فَمِنْ أَيْنَ لي
أَنْ أَدْرِيَ أَيْنَ
وَأَنا لا أَكادُ أَعْرِفُ –
– في عِزِّ نَهاري –
مَكْمَنَ قَلَمي أَيْنَ!

٢٠٠٤/١٠/١٠

154

# Where

Poetry hides
somewhere
behind the night of words
behind the clouds of hearing,
across the dark of sight,
and beyond the dusk of music
that's hidden and revealed.
But where is it concealed?
And how could I
possibly know
when I am
barely able,
by the light of day,
to find my pencil?

10.X.2004

# رِيتِك مَا تْصَرِّفِيهَا

هَا أَنَذا في المَوْقِع ذاتِهِ
لكِنَّ المَكانَ لَيْسَ تُرابًا وَفَضاءً
وَلَيْسَ حِجارَةً .
أَيْنَ اللَّوْزُ الأَخْضَرُ؟
أَيْنَ الشَّحيتيّاتُ والثُّغاءُ؟
أَيْنَ رُمَّانُ الأُمْسِياتِ
وَرائِحَةُ الخُبْزِ؟
أَيْنَ الْقَطا والشَّبابيكُ؟
أَيْنَ رَفَّةُ جَديلَة أَميرَة؟
أَيْنَ السَّمَّانُ
وَصَهيلُ المُحَجَّلاتِ
مَطْلوقاتِ اليَمينِ؟
أَيْنَ أَعْراسُ السُّنونو؟
أَيْنَ أَعْيادُ الزَّيْتونِ؟
وَفَرَحُ السَّنابِلِ؟
أَيْنَ أَهْدابُ الزَّعْفَرانِ
وَمَلاعِبُ الغُمَّيْضَةِ؟
أَيْنَ قاسِم؟
أَيْنَ الزَّعْتَرُ؟
أَيْنَ الشُّوحَةُ؟
تَنْقَضُّ عَلى الدَّجاجاتِ
مِنْ عاشِرِ سَما . . .

156

# The Place Itself,
## or I Hope You Can't Digest It

And so I come to the place itself,
but the place is not
its dust and stones and open space.
For where are the red-tailed birds
and the almonds' green?
Where are the bleating lambs
and pomegranates of evening—
the smell of bread
and the grouse?
Where are the windows,
and where is the ease of Amira's braid?
Where are the quails
and white-footed fettered horses whinnying,
their right leg alone set free?
Where are the wedding
parties of swallows—
the rites and feasts of the olives?
The joy of the branching spikes of wheat?
And where is the crocus's eyelash?
Where are the fields we played
our games of hide-and-seek in?
And where is Qasim?
Where are the hyssop and thyme?
Where is the kite descending on chicks
from the heaven's heights,

فَتَصْرُخُ خَلْفَها الجَدَّةُ:
«أَخَذْتِ الرُزِّيّه
يا فاجري!
رِيتِكْ مَا تْصَرّفيها
يا بْعِيدي...
رِيتِكْ مَا تْصَرّفيها! »

٢٠٠٤/٤/١٦

as the old woman shouts at it:
"You took our speckled hen,
you whore!
I hope you can't digest it!
You there, in the distance:
I hope you can't digest it!"

16.IV.2004

# بَينَ النَومِ واليَقْظَة

هي، في أَحَدِ أَصباحٍ
أوائلِ أَيّامِ نِيْسان
من كلِ تتالي سِنيّ الثلاث
أو أَربعِ السّنوات الماضية
تَسْتَدعي ...
بِصوتِها نِصفِ النّائِم
مِن طريقٍ أمامَ بَيتنا
مُحِبّي الكُلَّاج
وعشّاق العَسَلْ :
« كُلَّاج وعَسَلْ نَحِلْ للبيع
كُلَّاجْ، عسلْ
عسلْ، كلَّاجْ . »

—

أنا، في فِرَاشِي
لا نَائمٌ أَقصى النومِ
ولا يقظتي تُحيقُ بِنَواحي اليقظة
أُدْمِنُ سَمَاعَ ندائِها الحَميم
أتوقَّعُه بِلَهْفَةٍ
أتَشَوَّقُ إليه .

—

# Between Sleep and Waking

She, on one of the mornings
in early April
over the course
of the past three of four years,
would call in her drowsy voice
from the street before our house
to connoisseurs of honey
and those who loved *kullahj:*
*"Kullahj and honey from the hive for sale!*
*Kullahj, honey—*
*honey, kullahj."*

      —

In bed,
but not completely asleep,
my wakefulness not yet having reached
the outskirts of waking,
I grew used to hearing
her warm, familiar voice,
which, impatiently, with longing
I had been expecting.

      —

بعد أَن انتظرتُها
دونَ جَدوى
طَوال صدورِ الغُرَّة
من أيّام هذا الشَهْر
نَجَمَ في وعْيي
أَني حُرِمْتُ
جنّة ذاك الشَّدوِ
في هذه السَّنة ؛
فَانْتابَتني الظُنون .

—

ولما وَقَعْتُ على أَنَّنا الآن
ما زِلْنَا في بَاحِة أيّام آذار
ضُمّخَ صَبَاحِي
بطيفِ صَوتها العذْب
نِصْف النّائم
القادِم بعد شَهرٍ:
أحسَسْتُ أنَّ سَنَا رَشْفة العَسَل
يَسْري، فِعلاً ، في رُوحي
وأَشْرَقَت بذاكِرَتي
نكْهةُ الكُلّاج إيّاها
فيما أَنا . . . كالعَادَة:
مُسْتيقِظٌ عَبَرَ بيَاض أَشْرعَة النّوم
نائمُ في ظلِّ لُجَّة اليَقْظة .

162

After I'd waited
for her in vain
throughout the first few
days of the month,
it began to appear
that this year I would be deprived
of the garden of that chant,
and doubts plagued me.

—

But when suddenly
it dawned on me
that we were still
in March's range
my morning was drenched in the specter
of her sweet, drowsy voice,
which in less than a month would reach me.
I felt that rays of the honey's brilliance
were actually flowing through my soul,
and in my memory there rose
the savor of *kullahj*,
while I…
as always, was waking
through the whiteness of the sail of sleep,
and sleeping… in the shadow of waking's wave.

# لَيْسَ إلاّ

اَلتَّغَيُّراتُ الَّتي تَعَرَّضْتُ لَها
في جَسَدي
بَعْدَ أَنْ وَضَعْتُ قَدَمي
في السِّتينات
مِنْ عُمْري
كانَتْ مَعْدودَةً وَعاديَّةً .
بِضْعُ تَغَيُّراتٍ، لَيْسَ إلاّ:
ضَغْطٌ يُضاغِطُ « سُكَّري »
اِلتِهابٌ مُقيمٌ في المَفاصِلِ .
اِضْطِرابٌ مُزْمِنٌ
في عُصاراتِ كَوْكَبَةٍ
مِنَ الغُدَدِ الأَساسيَّةِ .
فُضَّ فَمي
ثُقُلَ سَمَعي
خَلَلٌ جَذْريٌّ
في رُؤْيَتي عَبْرَ نَظّاراتٍ سَميكَةٍ .
اَلاعْتِمادُ الكُلِّيُّ عَلى العُكّازِ
حَتّى، عِنْدَما أَسْعُلُ .
أَرَقٌ مَجوسيٌّ لا يَخْمَدُ
في لَيْلٍ أَسْودٍ أَسْودٍ
أَطْوَلَ مِنْ شَعْرِ سِتّينَ غُولَةً .

# Nothing More

The changes facing my body
when I first set foot in my sixties
were normal.
There were only a handful, nothing more:
a battle between my sugar and blood,
persistent inflammation in joints,
and chronic trouble
with the fluids flowing
from the principal cluster of glands.
I held my tongue
as my hearing worsened,
and a serious flaw developed
in my vision, even through thick glasses,
along with a total dependence
on my cane, even when coughing.
An unrelenting,
Zoroastrian insomnia pursued me
on the blackest of nights—
longer than the hair of sixty ghouls.

بِضْعَةُ « تَغَيُّراتٍ »، كَما تَرى،

إلى جانِبِ وَهْنٍ دائِم

في عَضَلَةِ الفَرَحِ مِنْ قَلْبِي .


أَيْضًا، مُلاحَظَةُ حالاتٍ عامَّةٍ لافِتَةٍ :

مِنْ فِئَةِ اللُّجوءِ إلى اسْتِعْمالِ التَّعْبيرِ :

« فُضَّ فَمي »

بَدَلَ القَوْلِ :

« سَقَطَتْ أَسْناني . »


٢٠٠٤/٥/١

As you see, there were only a few—
apart from those involving
ceaseless fatigue in the muscle
charged with joy in my heart.

An interesting general condition
was also observed—
along the lines of my resorting
to using the expression
"I held my tongue,"
instead of saying:
"My teeth fell out."

1.V.2004

# جِداءُ جَميل، جارُنا في صَفّورِية

جَميل،
إِبْنُ عَمَّةِ والِدي،
جارُنا بِصَفّورْيِه،
تَزَوَّجَ ثَلاثَ زَوْجَاتٍ
لَمْ يُرْزَقْ مِنْهُنَّ
لا بِإِبْنٍ يَحْمِلُ اسْمَهُ
وَلا بِإِبْنَةٍ تُحْيِي مَواتَ
القَلْبْ.

جَميل، إِبْنُ عَمَّةِ والِدي،
جارُنا بِصَفّورْيِه،
عَنْزَتُهُ الشّامِيَّةُ الشَّقْراءُ
واسِعَةُ العَيْنَيْنِ طَويلَةُ الشَّعْرِ —
وَلَدَتْ لَهُ
وَلِزَوْجاتِهِ الثَّلاثِ
بَعْدَ عَوْدَتِه مِنَ الحَجِّ بِيَوْمَيْنِ
سِتَّةَ جِداءٍ تَوَائِمَ، لَيِّنَةٍ
حَريرُ أَنْفاسِها
يُذَكِّرُ بِطُفُولَةِ الكَوْنِ.

جِداءُ جَميل
مَخْلُوقاتٌ لَيْسَتْ مِنْ هذا العَالَمِ.
جِداءُ جَميل وَزَوْجاتِه

# The Kid Goats of Jamil

Jamil,
my father's cousin,
our neighbor in Saffuriyya,
married three wives
but had from them
neither a son to inherit his name
nor a daughter to refresh his heart.

Jamil, my father's cousin,
our neighbor in Saffuriyya,
owned a wide-eyed,
long-haired,
blond Damascene she-goat
that gave birth to six wooly kid goats
two days after he returned from Mecca;
their silken breath reminded you
of the childhood
of the world!

Jamil's kid goats
are creatures of another world;
Jamil and his three wives' kid goats

سِتُّ عَجائِنِ فَجْر
سِتُّ نُجَيْمَاتٍ فَارَّةٍ
مِنْ حَضانَةِ دَرَاري
لا يَهْدَأُ لَها ظِلٌّ .
يَغْفُو الحَجَرُ
تَنَامُ الشَّياطينُ
أَلشُّهُبُ والأَسْمَاكُ تَنَامُ
وَجداءُ جَميل لا تَنْعَسُ .

تَخْلُدُ لِرَاحَتِها الرِّيَاحُ
وَجداءُ جَميل لا تَتْعَبُ .
تَتَسَوَّرُ قَوْسَ البَوَّابَةِ
تَعْلُو أَكْوَامَ الحَطبِ
تَعْدُو عَلى حَفَّةِ السُّورِ إلى السَّطْحِ
تَجري في البَاحَةِ، في المَمَرْ:
بَيْنَ الرِّوَاقِ
وَبَيْنَ مَخْزَنِ الغِلَّة
فَتَذُوبُ أَلْوانُ فِرَائِها الزَّاهِيَةِ
في جَذَلِ حَرَكَاتِها المَرِحَةْ

يُجَنُّ جُنونُ جداءٍ جَميل
في عَشِيَّاتِ اخْضِرَارِ اللَّوْزِ .
وَمَعَ أَوْبَةِ قَمَرِ الحَصَادِ
تَقْفِزُ جداءُ جَميل وَزَوْجَاتِه
مِنْ شَبَابيكِ جُلُودِها،
تَتَأَرْجَحُ، تَثِبُ، تَرْقُصُ
في فِضَّةِ نَشْوَةِ الدُّنْيَا

are six dough-smooth figures of dawn,
six baby stars escaping
the nursery of a star-filled sky.
Their shadows won't stand still.

Stones sleep,
Satan sleeps,
shooting stars and fish sleep,
but Jamil's kid goats never tire.
The wind rests,
but Jamil's kid goats
never grow drowsy.

They scale the archway,
leap over the log pile,
scramble up to the roof's edge,
and run around in the courtyard,
then down the path
between the storeroom
and the goat shed.
Their frisky movements dissolve
their coats' gay colors.

Their craziness simply goes crazy
on evenings when the almonds go green,
and with the return of the harvest moon.
The kid goats of Jamil and his wives
leap out of the windows of their skin.
They sway, pounce, and dance
in the silvery fullness of the world,

كَقَنَادِيلِ زِئْبَقٍ مُعَلَّقَةٍ
تُعَابِثُ أَسْلاكَها
جِراءُ عَفَارِيتْ .

أَلْجِدْيانُ الوَافِدَةُ
أَفْعَمَتْ قَلْبَ جَميل
وَقُلوبَ زَوْجَاتِه
بِبَهْجَةٍ نَادِرَةٍ .
أَشاعَتْ فَرَحًا مُتَفَائِلاً .
فَرَحًا مُخْمَلِيًا دَافِئًا
مَلأَ البَيْتَ والنُّفوسَ
غَمَرَ الرِّواقَ والمَمَرَّ
وَعَطَّرَ مَخْزَنَ الغَلَّةْ!

أَلْغِبْطَةُ لَمْ تَكُنْ وَقْفاً
عَلى الزَّوْجَاتِ الثَّلاثْ
أَلحُبورُ لَمْ يَقْتَصِرْ
عَلى الشَّقْراءِ الشَّامِيَّةِ
ذاتِ العَيْنَيْنِ الوَاسِعَتَيْنِ
والقَلْبِ الذَّهَبِيّ؛
لَمْ يَكُنِ السُّرورُ مَرْهونًا بِجَميل
إِبْنِ عَمَّةٍ وَالِدي
جارِنا بِصَفُّورِيه –
«أَلفَرَحُ المُتَفائِلُ»
عَمَّ النَّاسَ
شَمِلَ البَلْدَة
كَنَشْوَةِ أَوَّلِ الغَيْثْ .

like dangling lamps of mercury
being tugged at by puppy-sized jinn.

The newly arrived kid goats
filled the hearts of Jamil and his wives
with a rare, buoyant splendor;
they warmed their spirits
and spilled soft as velvet
into their home,
into the goat shed and onto the path,
perfuming the storeroom.

That pleasure was never limited
to the three wives;
the gladness was never restricted
to the blond, wide-eyed,
long-haired,
golden-hearted Damascene she-goat;
the happiness was never confined to Jamil,
my father's cousin, our neighbor in Saffuriyya.
A bright, hopeful joy
    spread out over the people,
        over the village,
    like the joy of the year's first rain.

# شَايٌ وَنَوْم

إِنْ كَانَ ثَمَّةَ مُدَبِّرٌ لِهَذَا الكَوْنِ
بِيَدِهِ البَسْطُ وَالقَبْضُ
بِأَمْرِهِ يُبْذَرُ البِذَارُ
وَبِمَشِيئَتِهِ يُحْصَدُ الحَصَادُ –
فَأَنَا أُصَلِّي لَهُ
طَالِبًا إِلَيْهِ :
أَنْ يَقْدُرَ أَجَلِي
حِينَ تَنْضُبُ أَيَّامِي
فِيمَا أَنَا جَالِسٌ
أَحْتَسِي مِنْ كُوبِيَ المُفَضَّلِ
خَفِيفَ شَايِهِ
طَفِيفَ حَلَاهُ
فِي ظِلِّ صَيْفٍ بَعْدَ ظُهْرِي الحَمِيمِ.
وَإِذَا لَمْ يَكُنْ شَايٌ وَظُهْرٌ
فَإِبَّانَ نَوْمَتِي العَذْبَةِ
بُعَيْدَ الفَجْرِ.

—

أَمَّا جَزَائِي
إِنْ كَانَ لِي أَنْ أَرَى الجَزَاءَ،
أَنَا الَّذِي لَمْ أَبْقُرْ
فِي عَاجِلَتِي

# Tea and Sleep

If, over this world, there's a ruler
who holds in his hand bestowal and seizure,
at whose command seeds are sewn,
as with his will the harvest ripens,
I turn in prayer, asking him
to decree for the hour of my demise,
when my days draw to an end,
that I'll be sitting and taking a sip
of weak tea with a little sugar
from my favorite glass
in the gentlest shade of the late afternoon
during the summer.
And if not tea and afternoon,
then let it be the hour
of my sweet sleep just after dawn.

—

And may my compensation be—
if in fact I see compensation—
I who during my time in this world

بَطْنَ نَمْلَةٍ
لَمْ أَسْلُبْ مالَ قاصِرٍ
وَلَمْ أُزَوِّرْ مِكْيالَ زَيْتٍ
لَمْ أَهْتِكْ سِتْرَ سُنونُوَّةٍ
وَلَكَمْ أَضَأْتُ
مَقامَ سَيِّدِنا
شِهابِ الدّينِ
في لَيالِي الجُمَعِ.
وَما اسْتَهْدَفْتُ قَطْ
أَنْ أَكونَ الغالِبَ في لَعِبٍ
مَعَ جارٍ أَوْ مَعَ صَديقٍ
أَوْ حَتّى مَعَ أَحَدِ المَعارِفِ.
لَمْ أَسْرِقْ قَمْحًا
لَمْ أَنْهَبْ ماعونًا
فَبِوُدّي:
أَنْ يُقَيَّضَ لي
أَنْ أَلْمَحَ مَرَّةً كُلَّ شَهْرٍ
أَوْ كُلَّ شَهْرَيْنِ
تِلْكَ الّتِي حُرِمْتُ مِنْ رُؤْيَتِها
مُذْ فارَقْتُها
في صَدْرِ عُمْري.

—

أَمّا الطَّيِّباتُ في الآجِلَةِ
فَحَسْبِيَ مِنْ لَذّاتِها
الشّايُ وَالنَّوْمْ!

٢٠٠٤/٩/٢٧

didn't split open an ant's belly,
and never deprived an orphan of money,
didn't cheat on measures of oil
or violate a swallow's veil;
who always lit a lamp
at the shrine of our lord, Shihab a-Din,
on Friday evenings,
and never sought to beat my friends
or neighbors at games,
or even those I simply knew;
I who stole neither wheat nor grain
and did not pilfer tools
would ask—
that now, for me, it be ordained
that once a month,
or every other,
I be allowed to see
the one my vision has been denied—
since that day I parted
from her when we were young.

But as for the pleasures of the world to come,
all I'll ask
of them will be—
the bliss of sleep, and tea.

27.IX.2004

# So What (a story)

### 1

I went barefoot the first ten years of my life, and while I was bitter about being deprived of shoes, and my incessant desire to get hold of a pair overwhelmed me, my suffering on the day the Moroccan shoeseller came to our village—on that day alone, by God—my suffering on that single day was such that it surpassed the torment I'd suffered at having gone barefoot for all of the ten previous years.

### 2

But I should explain what I mean right away, lest one understand from this that my despair at having gone barefoot throughout the years that preceded the arrival of the Moroccan involved only fleeting, superficial feelings, free of any real misfortune or distress; for in fact, much as I try, I can barely begin to describe the damage done to me by the glances of the neighborhood boys, and the neighborhood men, and the neighborhood women, and even the glances aimed my way by young neighborhood girls who hadn't yet left the eggshell.

These looks from the children, in particular, struck with more power against my flesh and bones and blood, and burned more fiercely against my heart and spirit and nerves, than the hot embers of soil and sand beneath the soles of my feet in the scorching heat of summer. I'll never forget the words of our math teacher, who may have believed that my going barefoot was a kind of hobby I pursued with my father's encouragement—those words which in one way or another surfaced in the course of nearly every math lesson, words which, even at the height of summer, have always recalled for me the bite of frost-covered ground in the early hours of a winter day:

"What are we going to do with you, Khalid? Tell your father I'd like to see him. Tell him, for me, will you, a little manners wouldn't hurt."

All this, to say nothing of the thorns sharp as venomous stingers, and the stones of the roads and the paths, and the edges of the court-yard and threshing-floor pebbles pointed like the tips of nails... and apart from the daggers of splintered glass, which carried out their skillful work on my feet, slicing, splitting, slashing as I played or jumped about, and as I raced around, now chasing my rivals and now running away from them. My mother would scream and scold me, especially as she took hot ashes from the oven or the brazier and applied them to a new and "serious" wound with which I'd just returned...

She'd wrap my injured foot in an old rag cut from what once had been a piece of my sister Amneh's clothes—its color, as I re-member it, once was green, and if it wasn't green, then most likely it was red. And then she would bind the rag with twine, tighter and tighter, till it held fast and I shrieked, the pain was so fierce. Mother would shout at me, her reproachful anger never entirely free of her sad and deep compassion, "You deserve it! You mischievous little boy. Haven't I told you a thousand times: Stop playing these games of yours."

"What can I do? I swear, I didn't see it... I was on my way home... a sharp piece of rusty iron stabbed me!"

3

No, this sense I had of being subject to an ordeal wasn't just fleeting and superficial; on the contrary, it made me miserable, and I was continually suffering on its account, always looking at shoes on the storefront shelves and on other people's feet, despairing of ever getting hold of a pair of my own. I listened to the teacher's icy pearls of wisdom, and my teeth chattered; I gave in to the treatment for my wounds, to the hot ashes and the suffering, to absorbing the stares from behind me and before me and beside me, as I sank into the bog of my agonizing shame. Oddest of all was the fact that the stares of the men and boys were one thing, but the stares of the girls were quite another. May God so love me that He one day allows me to return the favor to those skinny little know-nothings who couldn't tell right from left, or the bleats of their mothers from the calls of the market fishmongers.

And so I would go into our house in the middle of a fiercely cold or unbearably hot day, and point to my two bare, swollen feet, redder than sore and bloodshot eyes. I would open my mouth, about to complain, my complaint paving the way for my request from my mother for a pound for shoes on sale in one of the storefront dis-lays… But I would soon understand that my arrival had interrupted a talk between my father and mother—my father continuing on in his hoarse, lowered voice, and this before I could finish my complaint and find the words to ask for the money: "Like I told you, go to Abu Abbas, and tell him to sell it to us on credit. Tell him. He'll give you a two-piastre can of tomato paste… He'll sell it to us on credit."

My mother would answer, pleading with him, "Please, you go, or send Khalid… Here he is now…"

I would swallow my complaint, gulp down my request, and shut my mouth on what suddenly seemed hotter than embers and more bitter even than wormwood.

4

All this is entirely true. But the truth of truths is also that what hurt me and made me miserable throughout these ten barefoot years came to a head on the day of the incident of that Moroccan's shoes. It was gathered, condensed, concentrated, and intensified, added to and compounded until it turned into a frightening nightmare that the mind cannot possibly envision or the imagination contain… It aroused such mythical terror that day was turned into night for me, and the light was strewn with darkness, and sleep crept into my wakefulness. It happened in a single day, or more accurately, on just one late afternoon of a single day, indeed I might say that it came into existence, took shape, and revealed its power, like an explosion, within a single, distinct moment. My bitterness over not having had any shoes and my desire to acquire them were suddenly joined in a deep-seated burning that surpassed, in one brief instant, all I had suffered in the ten barefoot years combined.

5

The thing I remember now, and which seems so strange to me that I barely believe it happened, is that the incident didn't at first make much of an impression on me. It was of no special interest and aroused no unusual concern. I didn't stop running around when the neighborhood boys I was playing with after the afternoon prayers that day began to spread the word: the wandering shoe salesman from Morocco had come to the village, he and his horse, and he had amazing children's shoes—unbelievably beautiful, elegant, and inexpensive shoes—which he was hoping to sell in advance of the upcoming holiday. No, I didn't stop playing to run off with the other children toward the Moroccan, who had set up shop at the square across from the mukhtar's guesthouse in order to display the fine children's shoes he was offering.

It may have been despair, or despondency, that shaped my response. Or maybe it was simply a matter of my being utterly helpless in the face of the situation, or perhaps it all came back to my indifference and apathy, which in turn sometimes evolved from my despondency and helplessness and despair… The result was: I didn't run. And why should I? What good would my running there have done? What had changed? I was well aware that my barefoot condition couldn't be traced to an absence of shoe salesmen in the village. In fact, more than one store sold shoes, and one of the villagers even made them and would, with great pleasure, offer a pair to anyone willing to part with his pound and a half, or two. How many times had I passed the fine-looking shoes stacked on the shelves in the stores or set out in a row on their thrones in the small storefront window of Hamza's shop, where there were shoes whose colors ranged from the deep-red of twilight to a black that glimmered like starlings' wings to a dark chocolate brown—and also shoes whose two brilliant, marvelous tones enthralled the eye and truly enchanted the mind!

No, shoes of assorted colors and numerous kinds were plentiful enough in the village. They were, as they say, at hand. The problem, so far as I was concerned, was that they would never be *at foot*. In fact, I believed that the shoes would never really be within rocket range of my feet. My problem, which had neither solution nor resolution, and in the face of which I was helpless, lay in the principle of "forbidden fruits" or the law of "cash and carry," which governed one's dealing with shoes in general, whether it came to the stores in the village or to the Moroccan's saddlebags. It made little difference whether the merchant was from North Africa or the East or a nearby village, or even, should God so will it, from China. Why should I run? Why should I race toward what would inevitably lead to nothing more than a renewal of my bitterness? Did it matter that it wouldn't be a local bitterness, but a fresh, imported, exotic one from the distant land of our brothers in the Maghreb?

I didn't run. I kept on playing my hopscotch, or looking for another scarab in another pile of dirt. For the Moroccan, as I recall the incident now quite well, woke in me at first no special interest or any unusual concern.

## 6

Moreover, for almost a year before the Moroccan's arrival, I had started to grow tired of dreaming in front of the shoe-store displays. I would stand there looking, but without prolonging my gaze or lingering. A short stop, a glance or two, and then I would turn my back on the shoes and the grief and the heartache they brought on. I even started to ignore the price tags, and would read neither yesterday's crossed-out figures nor today's reduced prices. A short stop, a shorter look, and I'd be on my way, either to play with my friends or—if it was threshing season—to go to the threshing floor that belonged to one of our relatives. I'd take a short, wild ride on the threshing-board pulled by his wonderful chestnut horse, or get off and go down to the fields to trap small birds and partridges with a snare I had made with my own two hands from old wires and ribs of discarded umbrellas.

If it was winter and rainy, I would take advantage of the breaks between showers, roll up my hem to the knee, and plunge my feet into the water of one of the canals until they exhausted the depths of the channel and reached bottom. I would balance the timing of the movements of my upper-body and legs with the movements of my arms, open in the air like the wings of a bird, and start to walk with the water in the canal, which sometimes curved around and sometimes went straight, sweeping along with it rainwater from the neighborhood streets and roofs and alleys on its way to the vegetable gardens and the village fields... I'd walk, stand, then walk in the water, which usually covered my calf, feeling against my bare legs and the flesh of my feet and the nerve-ends of my toes small pieces of metal, for the most part little coins with holes at their center, coins that had been lost by their owners and swept away by the water, or marbles, bullet casings, and old ladies' copper rings that had been thrown away by grandsons, and small keys, and sometimes bigger keys, in addition to crooked old nails, bent like the words of liars.

Sometimes I would find pieces of colored Roman glass, three or four amazing crystal beads that the rain had kicked up and released from the prison where they had been hidden only a short while ago, the currents of water having pushed them along in the flow, so that as they wound around and floated along, as they were thrown up and down and swept away, in front of and then behind the current, they seemed to be dancing, rejoicing in their newfound freedom from their ancient Roman jail.

But my happiness was indescribable the day I stumbled across an old top, took off what was stuck to it, dried out its wood, and painted it with a blue ink, until it looked brand-new.

It's entirely possible that the joy I took in exploring, the pleasures of hunting and running around and playing, were experienced by none of the boys in the neighborhood in the same way that I experienced them, as most of them had shoes, something which denied them the delights of descending barefoot into the canal and feeling for things with their toes, and scooping them up skillfully from the water, and running back with them to the house, like a hero returning home with a prize—this, apart from my being almost absolutely convinced of the utter futility of my hope of ever owning a pair of shoes, now or at any time in the near future. Maybe all this was meant to keep me from having any sudden, jarring thoughts about shoes, or to keep my thoughts of them far from each other, to make sure they didn't act up, and to prevent any outbursts of longing. Sometimes, for a while or longer, all did in fact seem quiet—until, over the course of that year, I began to notice my tendency to reduce the amount of time I spent standing in front of the stores, and to shorten my stares at the shoes. I started making unconscious efforts as well to exclude the shoes from my field of attention, to push them back into the furthest reaches of my mind.

7

What I wasn't prepared for, by God, what I was not prepared for came to pass when the sun was a jinn's dark-red eye gliding toward the horizon, rushing, gazing down as it neared the moment of its plunge behind the western hills. The cloven hooves of livestock, and the uncloven hooves of the other animals, and the feet of the farmers and shepherds returning from the pastures and fields raised up dust between the late-afternoon and twilight, and gray, burnt-looking clouds grew gloomy, hovering over the entrance to the village like clouds of smoke over the tents of kidnappers and Gypsy thieves of pots and pans, shoes and lambs. It was just at this time that one of the neighborhood boys, Salim Amun, came and said something that made me throw down what was in my hand and ask him with a sigh of disbelief:

"Are you saying shoes for twenty piastres?"

Salim Amun answered, and I felt the sincerity of his words and the look in his eyes, the purest trust flowing from his lips:

"Yes, the Moroccan's shoes are only twenty piastres. It's incredible. If you don't believe me, go and see for yourself."

I rushed off, leaping higher than I'd ever imagined I could leap... And so I arrived at the mukhtar's square.

After two additional surprising leaps, which startled the sorrel horse tied by its halter to a wooden peg driven into the ground some four or five meters from its owner, I found myself standing over the shoes, stroking them in my mind as I turned them over and over in my imagination. My concentration wasn't at all disturbed by the horse, which reared up on its back legs, raising its forelegs over its head, as it sent out the whinny of a strange, frightened animal. I paid no heed to the wearied voice of the man and the dried-up words he directed at his horse in order to calm it down. I didn't even look at the man's face, or notice his features. It was the shoes alone that occupied me. The shoes alone. Or what remained of the shoes that had been on display, spread out in a row on the flattened saddlebags on the ground before the squatting Moroccan, who was skinny and had a thick, black beard. The man would have held no interest for me at all, if it weren't for the fact that he was selling beautiful children's shoes for twenty piastres a pair. Only twenty piastres. No, the shoes themselves were what occupied me and made me oblivious to everything else in the square.

When I asked the man if what Salim Amun had told me was true, he assured me, in his Moroccan dialect:

"That's correct, a pair for twenty francs."

"You mean, *a pair of shoes* for twenty *piastres?*" I asked the man, and he answered:

"That's right, twenty piastres. We say francs. Yes, a pair of shoes for twenty piastres."

8

I don't know how I got home: I ran with such speed and power that my feet barely touched the ground. The clouds of dust, burnt by the summer heat, were still riding over one another and lengthening continuously, as the caravans and herds advanced in the direction of the minaret and the upper part of the village, penetrating and crawling slowly toward the eastern olive groves. My mother was alone in the courtyard, and Father joined us when he heard me burst into tears and say:

"Shoes for twenty a pair. Hurry before they're gone. Hurry, only twenty piastres a pair."

My mother said, sadly: "God help you, my child." I interrupted her with my pleading, and my father backed her up with his silence, completing her expression without having to utter a word. I cried out—for I, more than anyone, knew just what that help would be, and my cry mixed with my bitter weeping and my weeping bled into my beseeching scream:

"Only twenty piastres, hurry, before they're gone, by God, or I'll throw myself into the well. Just twenty piastres."

And suddenly... a new page was turned. Mother drew near to Father and I heard her tell him: "...from Abu Abbas, and Emm Qasim... and I have eight." My father left for Abu Abbas's store, and my mother called out to Emm Qasim, our neighbor, from whom we were separated by a waist-high wall of piled-up stones.


9


I flew on enchanted wings! Where are you, O my Moroccan?! I flew toward the thin old man with the black beard and the saddle-bags laid out beneath the pairs of shoes that awaited me... I was flying, and my mind began to fathom the secrets of flight, or at least the flight of children, and I grasped my twenty piastres tightly in my hand, being careful lest they slip out between my fingers. My feet lapped up the distance, and I soared.

The sun had set, and the dust had settled on the rocks of the foothills and the oak branches. The mukhtar's square was now utterly silent and still. There was no movement within it, not a sound, not a breeze, and this time the horse wasn't startled by my arrival. I observed that the Moroccan demonstrated no particular anticipation of a new buyer who might bring him an additional sale. He paid no attention to my appearance, and didn't seem to notice me standing there suddenly before him. In his right hand the man was holding two brown shoes. He was in the process of putting them into one of the saddlebags, which he grasped with his left hand. I spoke up, my breathing still heavy from the race to the square:

"Take the twenty piastres and give me the shoes!"

"There aren't any left."

After some effort, I understood that he was telling me that nothing remained for me now, and I said to him, gesturing toward his right hand:

"That pair! Sell them to me. Here's the money."

And the man said to me, his words full of warm regret:

"But sir, these are no good, they're both for the right foot. They're useless."

"What do you mean, useless? Give them to me and take the twenty."

The man put the two brown shoes on the ground, and pointed to the toe of one of the two shoes, and then moved the gesture to the toe of the other. With a voice like thin copper wire, a voice that contained, it seemed to me, equal parts of my father's grief and my mother's sadness, and more than a few figures of speech that I did not understand, he started to explain the problem to me. From the movement of his lips and his gestures, and from his sorrowful tone, I understood what I could no longer avoid—the two shoes were each for the right foot, and no other shoes remained. I had come too late.

I gave no thought to the disadvantages of having two right shoes, or, for that matter, to the advantage of two lefts, and didn't enter into any complicated calculations. I neither thought nor hesitated, but said to the man straightaway:

"Right, right... so what? Sell me the two shoes and I'll take care of the rest."

"But two right shoes aren't good for you. You can't walk with them."

"So what! What difference does it make whether they're right or left? It's none of your business. Sell them to me, and it's a deal—that's that."

"They're both rights."

"So what! Sell them to me and don't worry about it."

After several rounds of this back-and-forth—the man saying "two rights are useless" and me repeating "so what," we ended up at the two takes: he took the twenty piastres and went off to the mukhtar's guesthouse, and I took the two right shoes and set off running for home!

10

The weather was stifling, the air ungiving, the voices of the people, farm animals, and dogs were still, and I—I simply couldn't believe that I'd actually gotten hold of my shoes! As I approached the house, I imagined that the best way to conceal the two right shoes from the eyes of my father and mother was to put them on outside, and then, somehow, they would shift from the realm of two singles into the realm of being a pair... And so, with my new pair of shoes I'd enter the courtyard. After I'd taken a few steps, I'd come into our room where my parents couldn't help but see me, and, with the new brown shoes on my feet, I'd parade before them, like the other people God created, and hear them say: "Congratulations! God bless you." And I would respond: "May you be blessed..." And they would notice nothing unusual.

That's how I pictured it.

Counting on this scenario, I stood at the entrance to the court-yard and put the shoes on the ground, then stepped into them. I raised my right foot and put it down to take a firm step on the stone threshold of the courtyard, and then it was my left foot's turn… I raised it up and sent it out to complete my first step toward the entrance, and, I don't know how, I stumbled and somehow fell to the ground.

I rose right away, my heart pounding wildly, and I tried to take another step. The right foot went well, and I put it where I wanted it. The left, however, filled me with terror—and before executing the step this time, I cautiously approached the hard, level ground before me, which was empty of all that might trip one up. I moved my foot wisely, and raised it slowly and deliberately, and lowered it with great care, but, nevertheless, when my foot felt the ground and sensed I was standing securely on it and completing the line… again it slipped and I stumbled. This fall was worse than the first. I landed on a harder spot, and the sound I produced brought my parents out of the house bareheaded and alarmed. They saw me stretched out flat, my forehead touching the ground.

My father rushed to lift me up, and my mother cried out anxiously:
"What happened to you, my dear? What happened? God protect you… What happened?"
I told her, and the taste in my mouth wasn't far from that of salty earth:
"It's nothing, nothing, it's over. Nothing happened."
"What do you mean nothing?" said my father, taking hold of my hand… And before I could think to try walking again, my father lowered his gaze from the small spot of warm blood on my lower lip to my new brown shoes:
"Khalid!" My father said sternly. "Take off those shoes!"
Trembling, I said:
"But, Papa… why should I take them off?"
"They're both for the right foot. Take them off!"
"So what? What difference does it make?!"

"Take them off! Don't make me get angry at you!"

My father started to list the reasons for me, explaining how it wasn't possible to walk with shoes like these. My mother supported him:

"The man tricked you, my dear… Go and return them."

"Why should I return them?!"

"They're two rights."

"So what?"

And my father bellowed:

"Take them off!"

I starting sobbing, removing my new brown shoes, and I sobbed on my way back to the mukhtar's square, and I sobbed telling my story to the Moroccan with the thin build and the black beard, who gave me back the twenty piastres with what seemed an apology:

"I told you they weren't good for anything."

## 11

The following morning, while I wasn't really sleeping and yet not entirely awake, my face was still buried in the feathers of my pillow, wet with the acid mix of sweat and tears. My head pounding continuously with the rhythm of my rapid, disturbed pulse, hot with its hammering, I heard the voice of my mother—like the voice heard in a dream, brushing up against the outer shell of my consciousness but not quite settling into memory. It came to me from our side of the waist-high wall of piled-up stones. Mother was talking to our good neighbor, Emm Qasim, returning the five piastres she had borrowed from her the day before, and thanking her.

"Bless you for your kindness, Emm Qasim. We didn't need them, neighbor. God bless you a thousand times over. May God let us repay you for your favor. By God, Emm Qasim, Khalid's eyes barely closed last night. He was hot as fire all night long, my sweet child… every few minutes he'd start up with a fright and scream: 'So what?!' He'd seem to sleep for two minutes, and then he'd start up and cry out again: 'So what?! So what?! So what?!'"

# Notes

A NOTE ON THE TRANSLATION, PP. XXIII–XV

The poet Adonis has written about the etymology of the word *sha'ir* in *Arab Poetics*, trans. Catherine Cobham (University of Texas Press, 1990), pp. 57–58.

Shammas recently published a collection of Taha Muhammad Ali's work in Hebrew translation (Andalus, 2006).

The Tolstoy passage is from "What Is Art," trans. A. Maude, in *The Portable Tolstoy*, ed. John Bayley (Penguin, 1978), p. 837.


P. 5

labneh: A soft white cheese made from strained yoghurt.


P. 77

*Sada'*: A legendary bird that rises from the skulls of the slain whose blood has not been avenged.


P. 137

mihrab: The niche at the front of the mosque indicating the direction of Mecca, and thus the direction of prayer.


P. 139

Badawy: A thirteenth-century Muslim saint, said to have performed miracles both while alive and from his Egyptian tomb.


P. 143

fellah: Arabic for "peasant," which indicates an ethos.

P. 161
*kullahj*: A phyllo pastry filled with farmer cheese and doused with syrup.

P. 177
Shihab a-Din: Saladin's nephew, whom legend holds to be the liberator of Nazareth from the Crusaders.

P. 182
mukhtar: Official head of the village.

# About the Author and Translators

TAHA MUHAMMAD ALI is the author of four volumes of poetry in Arabic and a collection of short stories. He operates a souvenir shop in Nazareth.

PETER COLE's most recent collection of poems is *What Is Doubled: Poems 1981–1998*. He has published many volumes of translations from medieval and contemporary Hebrew, and has received numerous awards for his work, including the PEN Translation Prize, a *TLS* Translation Prize, and fellowships from the NEA, the NEH, and the Guggenheim Foundation.

YAHYA HIJAZI was raised in Jerusalem's Old City. A project consultant at the Palestinian Counseling Center and lecturer in the Department of Education at the David Yellin College, he has also worked as a teacher of Arabic and as a facilitator on projects bringing together Arab and Jewish communities in Israel and Palestine.

GABRIEL LEVIN's books include two collections of poems, *Sleepers of Beulah* and *Ostraca*, a prose work, *Hezekiah's Tunnel*, and translations from the Hebrew of Yehuda Halevi and S.Y. Agnon, and from the French of Ahmed Rassim. His work has appeared in the *TLS, PN Review, Agenda, Parnassus*, and many other journals.

www.ingramcontent.com/pod-product-compliance
Lightning Source LLC
Jackson TN
JSHW011935131224
75386JS00041B/1396